The Classroom Teacher's Guide to Supporting Students with

Dyslexia

The Classroom Teacher's Guide to Supporting Students with Dyslexia

(And Helping All Readers Along the Way)

MARK WEAKLAND

Routledge
Taylor & Francis Group
NEW YORK AND LONDON
A Stenhouse Book

Designed cover image: Getty Images

First published 2026
by Routledge
605 Third Avenue, New York, NY 10158

and by Routledge
4 Park Square, Milton Park, Abingdon, Oxon, OX14 4RN

Routledge is an imprint of the Taylor & Francis Group, an informa business

ISBN: 9781041014522 (pbk)
ISBN: 9781003618478 (ebk)

DOI: 10.4324/9781003618478

Typeset in Adobe Garamond Pro
by KnowledgeWorks Global Ltd.

To the researchers and the teachers—two sides of the same coin.

Contents

Acknowledgments

I want to acknowledge and thank the following folks: my sister, Dr. Melissa Weakland, who years ago encouraged me to focus on dyslexia as a topic of study; my immediate and extended family, who love to read and talk reading; my mother, Lynne, who was my original thought partner when it comes to reading instruction; Terry Thompson, who is a wonderful editor and a person who gets things done in the world; Michael Herzberg, development director at the Bureau of Education and Research, who gave me the opportunity to more thoroughly understand dyslexia and then take that understanding to teachers; and Dr. Richard Gentry, who inspired me to dive more deeply into how reading, writing, and spelling develop and interact.

Introduction

As teachers of reading, we have all been, at times, surprised and perplexed by a subset of students who should be easily learning to read but aren't. In my years as a special education teacher and reading interventionist, I puzzled over these children many times. In my first years of teaching, in charge of a self-contained learning support program for fourth and fifth graders, I typically had fifteen to sixteen students on my roster. Of those kids, two or three had an Individualized Education Program (IEP) that said "specific learning disability" and a profile of traits that looked like this: intelligent, hardworking, knowledgeable about the world, terrible at spelling, and very slow to make gains toward fluent reading. Have you had students like these in your classroom?

No one ever told me these students had *dyslexia*—neither parent nor school psychologist—and the term was not to be found on any educational record. Truth be told, I rarely thought about dyslexia during my early years of teaching because hardly anyone used the term. But looking back, I'd bet the remaining hairs on my head that numerous students in my special ed classroom had the condition.

Later, I co-taught a general education program specifically designed to boost the literacy growth of low-achieving third graders. Typically, in each year's cohort, three or four children needed intensive teaching to reach important benchmarks and achieve at least a year's worth of growth in reading. At this point in my career, I knew a bit about dyslexia, and I suspected my most struggling readers had it. But as in my special ed classes, none of the kids bore the label and only one had been assessed for it.

As the years rolled by and I continued to work with students and school systems, I came to understand a lot about the many factors that cause and contribute to reading difficulties. And in the last decade, much of my learning has focused on dyslexia: what it is, how it arises, and how to teach students who have it. In these years, I've discovered numerous misunderstandings regarding the condition; three are important to mention up front.

First, it is a mistake to think dyslexia arises solely from one or two variables. Dyslexia is rooted in the structure and performance of the human brain, an organ of immense and nuanced complexity. In addition, the condition itself is affected by multiple nonbiological factors, such as language, culture, and society. So, while dyslexia seems to be rooted in the less-than-optimal functioning of a few brain processing systems, whether the condition actually manifests, and if it does, how severely it affects a student depends upon a complex mix of brain structure subtleties and myriad "outside" elements.

A second misunderstanding is this: only highly trained specialists using specific programs can help students with dyslexia overcome their reading difficulties. The truth is we can all play a part in helping children who have dyslexia, and the practices used to teach them are often the *same* practices used to teach all children foundational literacy skills.

Finally, it would be an error to think that all teachers-in-training or all current teachers engaged in professional learning are well-versed about dyslexia. Rather, many educators still lack practical information about what dyslexia is and, importantly, how to teach students who have it. Thus, this book!

As its title says, this is a guidebook, meaning it's shorter and more succinct than a typical professional book. And, though it's presented in an accessible question and answer format, you'll want to note it isn't exhaustive. Still, this book will answer many common questions, in a user-friendly way, while providing plenty of connections to outside sources, so you can explore whatever issue or topic you find most pressing or fascinating.

Overall, the book's goals are fourfold: 1) to generally educate you about dyslexia, 2) to help you teach students with dyslexia to read, write, and spell, 3) to give you ideas on how students with dyslexia can be made to feel more comfortable in classroom settings, and 4) to show you how the knowledge you gain about teaching students with dyslexia can be used to teach *all* students to read, write, and spell.

These goals speak to another important point: many aspects of dyslexia are still being debated, including whether it actually exists! Researchers regularly argue over studies, debate statistics and experimental designs, and insist that some concepts, such as development dyslexia, are poorly defined and largely unproven—even as others say no such thing (1). This arguing and debating is not necessarily negative; in fact, it's how science works.

But as teachers and stakeholders, you likely don't have time to take a deep dive into the debates. Nor can you wait for statistically acceptable degrees of scientific certitude to appear. Your students need help, right now, and the only way to help them is through action, right now. And so, I have done my best to survey the literature, avoid the deepest weeds and set aside the least supported beliefs, all in an effort to present a general consensus around what dyslexia is, how it affects learners every day, and how we can help these learners in the classroom, right now. Thankfully, I've found there are robust bodies of research that point convincingly to commonly agreed upon conclusions. For this book, I have worked to translate these conclusions into actionable ways to support students who have or may have dyslexia, as well as other students who find learning to read difficult, for a multitude of reasons.

It's an exciting time to be a reading teacher. Scientific studies are ongoing and giving us more information all the time. Neuroscience is regularly discovering cutting-edge information about foundational literacy skills. And the continuing efforts of dyslexia advocates—from parent groups to national organizations—constantly move us toward increased equity and justice for all. These developments not only help the students who are working to overcome the effects of their dyslexia but also inform how we can address the needs of the larger classroom. A true win-win.

Together, we can join the researchers, advocates, and teachers who are working hard to make the world of reading a more welcoming and livable place, especially for the children who struggle the most.

Let's get started!

End of Chapter Resources

1 Stein, John. 2023. "Theories about Developmental Dyslexia." *Brain Sciences* 13 (2): 208.

CHAPTER 1

Learning About Dyslexia

Simply put, dyslexia is a neurobiological difference that makes it difficult for a person to learn to read and engage in fluent reading. Students who have dyslexia may read slowly, make decoding errors, and misread simple words like *them* and *what*, all of which can limit their comprehension of text. In addition, students with dyslexia may have trouble spelling words that others spell quite easily. Or they may have problems "finding words" while talking, pausing as they "search" for the word they want to say.

When thinking about dyslexia, it's helpful to keep the word *difference* in mind. In many ways, every human being is like every other. Each person on the planet is a bipedal member of the homo sapiens club, shaped by millions of years of evolution and imbued with a common set of physical and mental features. But evolution, genetics, nurture, and culture shape us as individuals, too, and amazingly, every person is unique.

The term *neurodiversity* neatly captures the idea that all people exhibit a degree of variance, large to small, in their unseen brain wiring. This variance ultimately leads to differences in perception, cognition, and responses to information. For people with dyslexia, their neural pathway differences make it harder for them to learn to read. Dyslexia, however, must be understood as a condition that is shaped by factors other than just neural circuitry. Though neurological in origin, the developmental trajectory of dyslexia can be influenced by a range of emotional, social, and environmental factors, such as a person's economic background, emotional make up, and educational experiences (1).

In this chapter, we dive into the details of dyslexia, exploring ways to define it, the neural circuitry that gives rise to it, and common misconceptions that surround it.

What does the word *dyslexia* mean?

The word *dyslexia* is constructed from two Greek roots, *dys* and *lexis*. *Dys* means inadequate or difficult while *lexis* means word or language and so *dyslexia* literally means "difficulty with words."

Is there one official definition of dyslexia?

No.

There are *many* definitions of the term, put forth by numerous groups. Here are two from well-known dyslexia-based organizations, the first being The Yale Center for Dyslexia & Creativity, long associated with the well-known dyslexia researcher, Dr. Sally Shaywitz, and the second being the International Dyslexia Association (IDA), which has worked with others to craft a mutually agreed-upon explanation of dyslexia that several state education codes have adopted. Notice the similarities and differences between the two.

1 "Dyslexia is defined as an unexpected difficulty in learning to read. Dyslexia takes away an individual's ability to read quickly and automatically, and to retrieve spoken words easily, but it does not dampen their creativity and ingenuity... Scientific research shows differences in brain connectivity between dyslexic and typical reading children, providing a neurological basis for why reading fluently is a struggle for those with dyslexia" (2).

2. "Dyslexia is a specific learning disability that is neurobiological in origin. It is characterized by difficulties with accurate and/or fluent word recognition and by poor spelling and decoding abilities. These difficulties typically result from a deficit in the phonological component of language that is often unexpected in relation to other cognitive abilities and the provision of effective classroom instruction. Secondary consequences may include problems in reading comprehension and reduced reading experience that can impede the growth of vocabulary and background knowledge" (3).

My favorite definition, published early in 2024, comes from a team of researchers led by reading scholar, Maryanne Wolf. Written as seven principles, the definition gives a "comprehensive, dynamic conceptualization of dyslexia" (4) that is still easy to understand. Here it is in an abridged form; you can read the unabridged, more nuanced version by following the link provided.

Follow this QR code, scroll to the end of the article, and read the unabridged seven-point definition for yourself

1. Dyslexia is a unique organization of the human brain that confers both disadvantages and advantages.
2. The most common disadvantage is the unexpected difficulty in acquiring fluent reading, spelling, and/or comprehension.
3. The most predictive factors of dyslexia are weaknesses in the phonological components of language and the processes associated with naming speed.
4. Dyslexia manifests differently depending on what is most vulnerable in the reading circuit for any given language and writing system.
5. Both the risk for and the developmental course of dyslexia are influenced by social, emotional, and environmental factors.
6. Dyslexia should never be associated with a lack of intelligence, talent, or effort. When structured literacy instruction is provided as early as possible, individuals with dyslexia can learn to read and develop their full potential.
7. Dyslexia can change over time, particularly when the strengths and advantages are fostered alongside preventive factors that emphasize resiliency, persistence of effort, and respect for the potential of every individual (5).

The word dyslexia was first coined in 1887 by Rudolph Berlin, a German ophthalmologist who noticed that some of his patients had problems reading but had nothing wrong with their vision. Ahead of his time, he speculated that their difficulties were caused by some physical change in their brain (6).

What are some traits of people with dyslexia?

Dyslexia presents as a complex mix of behaviors, the core of which are related to learning to read and engaging in the act of reading. They include:

- inaccurate word reading, lack of automatic word recognition,
- poor decoding skills,
- slow word reading, lack of reading fluency,
- poor spelling ability,
- difficulty with phonological skills, such as generating words that rhyme or segmenting a word into discrete sounds (phonemes),
- difficulty matching the letters seen on a page with the sounds those letters make (difficulty mastering sound–letter associations),
- difficulty with rapidly identifying objects, colors, and/or letters.

Other traits sometimes, but not always, associated with dyslexia include:

- difficulty finding the right word while speaking, unexpected pauses during speech,
- trouble with directions, in other words not easily knowing left from right,
- a lack of organizational skills,
- persistent letter and word spelling reversals, even in the face of consistent instruction,
- difficulty mastering grammar concepts,
- difficulty attending to task, paying attention,
- poor vocabulary,
- difficulty in learning a second language.

Do all children and adults with dyslexia exhibit the same traits?

No.

Some people exhibit many traits while others exhibit just a few. And the traits don't necessarily overlap. For example, consider two third-grade children who have been diagnosed with dyslexia. One is a poor speller, a slow reader, has trouble attending to tasks, has difficulty figuring out left from right, and lacks the ability to rapidly name letters. The other student, who happens to be the same age and comes from a similar background, is an average speller, can stay on task, and can rapidly name letters but exhibits a surprising inability to learn how to read.

Is dyslexia a physiological or psychological condition?

The bundle of characteristics that we call dyslexia is rooted in neurodiversity, i.e. differences in the brain. Thus, dyslexia is physiological in nature (7, 8). It is not brought on by factors outside of the brain that influence a person's psychological state, such as a poor diet, lack of sleep, environmental distractions, stressful personal experiences, or traumatic events. Certainly, these outside happenings can make learning to read, write, and spell difficult. But dyslexia's starting point—the reason it arises—is a difference in the brain-based reading circuit.

It's important to note that psychology does *connect* to dyslexia and influence it, even when it is in no way its cause. For example, the condition of dyslexia can produce impactful emotions that create something similar to a negative feedback loop. When students find it difficult to learn the reading skills their classmates are easily mastering, they may experience anxiety, disappointment, and/or frustration. These feelings then make learning to read even *more* difficult.

What is the brain's reading circuitry and how does it relate to dyslexia?

The brain is a remarkable organ. Its billions of neurons and trillions of neuronal connections enable human beings to run, smell, add numbers, tell stories, consider the future, gossip about neighbors, ponder the meaning of life, and… read!

Many brain pathways, such as the ones that give rise to speech and emotion, have evolved over hundreds of thousands of years. These circuits naturally wire themselves (come into existence) during a typical child's development. In contrast, other circuits are relatively "young" and do not wire themselves. The brain circuitry that enables reading, writing, and spelling is an excellent example of this type of young circuit (9).

Dr. Mark Seidenberg has described the neural pathways that enable reading as "the eternal triangle." According to Seidenberg, the foundational reading circuit comes into being when three brain processing areas are connected: the **semantic processing area**, which has to do with meaning, the **phonological processing area**, which is all about processing the word sounds of a language, and the **orthographic processing area**, which has to do with recording of and permanently storing correct letter sequences or word spellings (10). The three points of the triangle are wired into a circuit through repeatedly teaching (and practicing) the building blocks of literacy, such as sound–letter relationships, encoding skills (spelling), decoding skills (phonics), and the comprehension of text (11, 12, 13).

There are many great things about the eternal triangle model [Figure 1.1] and one is we can use it to understand what dyslexia is and how it comes about. For example, a deficit in someone's phonological area may make it difficult to form stable sound–letter associations (14, 15). The converse is also true, because progress (or lack thereof) in hearing the sounds of words marches in step with identifying and writing letters (16). Speech pathologist and neuroscientist, Dr. Martha Burns, says that children with dyslexia have a "muddy map," meaning their ability to form sound–letter associations is compromised. In addition,

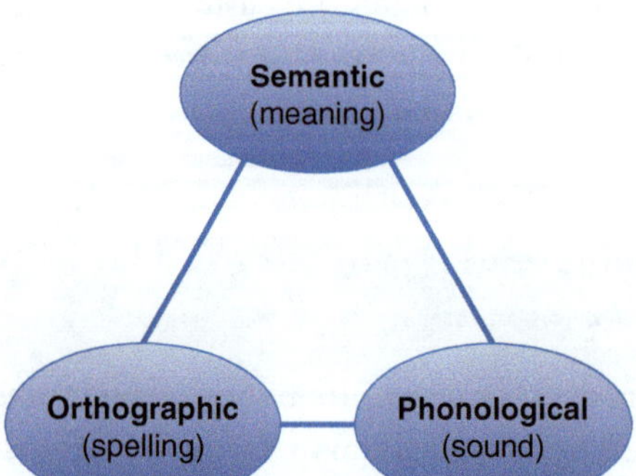

Figure 1.1 The Eternal Triangle: The Foundational Reading Circuit

a deficit in the orthographic area may lead to difficulties in rapid automatic word recognition, as well as troubles with "word finding" while reading (17). These traits – a lack of automatic word recognition, failure to accurately store and/or retrieve correct letter sequences, and difficulty with forming accurate sound–letter associations ("muddy map")—are hallmarks of many dyslexic students.

Once upon a time, there was no dyslexia. The ancient Sumerian people, whose civilization flourished between the Tigris and Euphrates Rivers (currently southern Iraq), developed the first alphabetic system for reading and writing somewhere around 6,000 years ago. Before this there were no written words and thus, no such thing as a reading difficulty.

What is the prevalence of dyslexia? Is it common or rare?

In my travels as a guest teacher, I often take a cab or Uber to my destination, at times striking up a conversation with the driver. Sometimes, when I mention that I'm speaking about dyslexia, the driver will remark, "You know, I think I have dyslexia!" If I probe a bit, asking why they think this is, the driver might say, "I had a hard time learning how to read," "I don't like to read," or "I'm a really lousy speller."

I mention this because although it's possible the drivers *do* have dyslexia, it's also possible they are confusing the terms *dyslexia* and *reading difficulty*. While dyslexia can be the origin of a reading difficulty, all reading difficulties are not caused by dyslexia (more on this later). In the United States, reading difficulties are sadly common. Dyslexia, however, is less so.

Determining who has dyslexia and who doesn't is tricky. Many factors influence who is ultimately identified (or not) and even a highly trained psychologist wouldn't dream of diagnosing dyslexia from the backseat of an Uber. In the United States, some researchers, such as Sally Shaywitz, say 20 percent of the general population has dyslexia (18). Meanwhile, the IDA gives a range, saying 15 to 20 percent of the population has a language-based learning disability, dyslexia being the most common (19).

Interestingly, the American Psychiatric Association (APA) gives the prevalence of dyslexia as 20 percent, with an estimated 5 to 15 percent of school-age children struggling with a learning disability such as dyslexia. The APA goes on to say that about 80 percent of these children have a reading impairment that *is* dyslexia, which translates to a school-age prevalence range of 4–12 percent (20).

Some organizations use a number within this 4–12 percent range. For example, an acquaintance of mine, who is associated with Pennsylvania's pilot program on dyslexia, told me that she and others use 10 percent as the prevalence rate. Similarly, the University of Michigan's website, *Dyslexia Help*, states "7–10% of the population is affected by dyslexia." But the site then goes on to say, "In the United States, NIH research has shown that dyslexia affects 5–10% of the population, with estimates as high as 17%" (21).

With all these numbers floating about, it's easy to see why prevalence remains one of the most common confusions about dyslexia. Right now the best we can say is that dyslexia affects 5–20 percent of the population and that its effects are distributed across this range, with some students displaying mild difficulties, others moderate, and some severe. When I share this information with audiences in my dyslexia seminars, I end by saying, "Dyslexia is less common than I once believed and more common than I sometimes think."

Does dyslexia exist in other languages?

Yes.

Although there is some debate about language systems that are logographic in nature, such as Chinese, the common consensus is that dyslexia occurs in people around the globe, regardless of the written language system they use (22). Knowing that dyslexia is neurobiological in nature, this fact makes sense.

Differences in rates of dyslexia, however, do seem to vary according to countries. For example, the prevalence of dyslexia in any English-speaking country can be influenced by that country's specific identification criteria (23). Widening the lens a bit, rates of dyslexia in English-speaking countries seem to be higher than in countries where people speak *transparent* languages, such as Spanish, Finnish, and Italian. Because the sound–spelling associations of these languages are relatively consistent and predictable (i.e. *transparent*), it is much easier to learn them, and this ease of learning can lead to lower rates of identified dyslexia, especially in the early grades of schooling (24, 25). Some studies suggest that in transparent language countries, like Spain, Finland, and Italy, about one person of every twenty (5 percent) is dyslexic (26). Again, this lower rate of dyslexia is due to the fact that the sound–letter associations of these languages are relatively straight forward and thus easier to learn, especially for students at risk of a reading difficulty for *any* reason (difference in brain wiring, growing up in poverty, attending a poorly functioning school system, etc.).

Is dyslexia inherited? Does it have a genetic component?

Yes, but with qualifications!

The neurobiological condition that is dyslexia is genetic in origin, meaning a child can inherit the condition from a parent. Two anecdotes illustrate this point:

- During my days as a reading specialist, when I met with parents to discuss their child's reading difficulty, it was not unusual for a parent to tell me, "When I was a kid, I had a really hard time learning how to read" or "My husband (or wife) is a lousy speller and a slow reader."
- In her Ted Talk on dyslexia, Kate Griggs, founder of the organization *Made by Dyslexia*, explains that she has dyslexia, her brother has dyslexia, her husband has dyslexia, and her two children have, you guessed it, dyslexia (27).

But it's always better to answer the question with research rather than anecdotes. Over decades, scientists have considered whether dyslexia is inheritable and if so, how much of it can be attributed to genetics. Studies cited by the National Institutes of Health (NIH) say a child whose parents are affected by dyslexia has a 40–60 percent chance of developing the condition. Additionally, the risk percentage increases when other family members are also affected and "twin studies have confirmed that genetic factors are substantially responsible for the familial clustering of dyslexia" (28).

It's clear that genetics give rise to dyslexia. But just how genetic information leads to it is still uncertain. One reason is that dyslexia seems to arise from the interactions of multiple genes. Unlike disorders propagated via a single gene (such as sickle cell anemia and cystic fibrosis), the multi-genetic nature of dyslexia makes it hard for researchers to identify specifically what is causing what. Some studies have begun to tease out chromosome regions and candidate genes and attempts are being made to link specific genes to specific traits, such as difficulty with rapid automatic naming. But current findings are by no means definite (29).

Another confounding factor is that reading ability and achievement is influenced by the environment (30). Imagine twins, separated at birth. Both carry the genes that make them susceptible to dyslexia. One child grows up in affluence, with few environmental stressors and a school that teaches reading well. In this case, the child might experience only mild reading difficulties and might never be diagnosed with dyslexia. In effect, their biological propensity toward developing a reading difficulty was tamped down or overcome by effective support systems. Meanwhile, the other twin grows up in poverty, lacks parental support, and goes to a school that doesn't teach reading effectively. In this scenario, the environment confers no protective advantages (quite the opposite) and the child might have trouble with reading and eventually be diagnosed with dyslexia.

Do more boys than girls have dyslexia?

Yes. But the answer has changed over time and thus needs some explanation.

We previously learned that determining the prevalence of dyslexia in the general population is tricky. Breaking it down into males and females is even more difficult. Also, there is the problem of new, correct information failing to replace old, incorrect information because humans tend to not want to let go of things, from long-held ideas thought to be true to tools and objects that no longer function as they should (a trait psychologists call *loss aversion*). The topic of reading disabilities among boys and girls is infused with both issues.

In previous decades, reading disabilities of *all types*, including dyslexia, were identified more often in boys than girls. But continued study revealed biases in these identifications (31). Then, in a 1990 study, as well as in her 2003 book, *Overcoming Dyslexia: A New and Complete Science-Based Program for Reading Problems at Any Level*, the influential researcher Dr. Sally Shaywitz posited there was *no* significant difference in the prevalence of dyslexia between boys and girls (32, 33). This idea continues to show up on websites, such as the University of Michigan's site,

Dyslexia Help, which states, "The actual prevalence of the disorder is nearly identical in the two sexes" (34).

This, however, is not the end of the story. With new information in hand and old research being reconsidered, our current understanding is that learning disabilities, including dyslexia, are more common in males (35, 36). There's a good chance this is due to differences in how the brains of boys and girls develop, as well as vulnerabilities unique to boys (37). In a 2022 YouTube video, neuroscientist and speech Pathologist, Dr. Martha Burns, says "The male brain matures at a different rate. It seems to be more vulnerable to neurodevelopmental factors, so males generally have more learning disabilities" (38).

Said another way, the brains of boys are in certain ways slower to develop than the brains of girls, which, in some situations, puts them at risk for not learning. Take, for example, two factors that correlate with reading skills and academic tasks: processing speed and impulse control. Boys and girls show significant differences in the development rates of both: by the age of five, girls show higher processing speed and more impulse control than boys (39). This gives girls an advantage in tasks that use processing speed (such as reading) and that benefit from impulse control (such as sitting in a seat and doing paper/pencil tasks). Conversely, boys, whose brains develop more slowly, have a greater chance of developing reading and spelling difficulties (later diagnosed as a learning disability) because their lower processing speed and levels of impulse control puts them at a disadvantage in learning-to-read situations.

Is dyslexia a medical condition?

No.

Dyslexia is not an illness or injury that can be medically treated or cured through an intervention like taking a drug or undergoing surgery. Rather, dyslexia is an underlying variance in how a person's brain operates, specifically when it comes to learning and engaging in reading. This variance cannot be erased (i.e. the neural circuitry of a student with dyslexia cannot be changed to exactly match that of a typically functioning reader). Rather, dyslexia is managed through adaptions and strategies and, to a certain extent, is overcome through effective literacy instruction that is direct, explicit, systematic, and intensive. Yes, a certain amount of "re-wiring" of the brain can take place through impactful teaching practices (40, 41). But because dyslexia is fundamental to a person's brain circuitry, elements of it will always be part of who a person is and how a person thinks and reacts, especially within the world of reading, spelling, and language.

Is dyslexia a *disorder* or a *disability*?

Specific learning disorder (or learning disorder) is a medical term used by the APA for a clinical diagnosis. It is an umbrella term that contains three specific learning disorders, all of which are neurodevelopmental in nature.

Learning disorders are characterized by a persistent impairment in at least one of three major areas – reading, written expression, and/or math. To be diagnosed with one, a child must meet four criteria: 1) have a difficulty in learning math and/or reading skills for at least six months and even with targeted help, 2) have academic skills substantially below what is expected for their age and causing problems in school, work, or everyday activities, 3) the difficulties start at school-age, and 4) the difficulties are not due to other conditions (such as a vision or hearing problem, an intellectual disability, an economic disadvantage, etc.) (42).

According to the APA, *dyslexia* is by far the most prevalent of the three disorders. An estimated 5 to 15 percent of school-age children struggle with a specific learning disorder and of these children, an estimated 80 percent have a reading disorder (commonly called dyslexia).

All learning disorders can vary in severity. This means a disorder like dyslexia exists on a continuum. Terms associated with the continuum are:

- *Mild*—Some difficulties with learning in one or two academic areas but may be able to compensate.
- *Moderate*—Significant difficulties with learning, requiring some specialized teaching and some accommodations or supportive services.
- *Severe*—Severe difficulties with learning, affecting several academic areas and requiring ongoing intensive specialized teaching

It's interesting that in their explanation and discussion of learning disorders, the APA uses *learning disorder* and *learning disability* interchangeably.

Meanwhile, the term *specific learning disability* (sometimes written as just *learning disability*) is often used by the educational and legal systems (43). Once someone, like a psychologist, has diagnosed a student as having a *learning disability*, that student has a federally designated identification that entitles them to certain legal protections and can qualify them for accommodations, services, and specially designed instruction in school, all of which are typically spelled out in an Individualized Education Program (IEP).

Finally, the term *learning difference* is gaining traction as a way to describe dyslexia. Because it doesn't label a child as "disordered" or "disabled" in any way, *learning difference* can be especially useful when speaking with students about their difficulties.

To summarize, depending on which organization you consult, dyslexia is considered a disorder, a disability, and a difficulty. And depending on who you are talking to, you can use any of the three to make your point.

What is *dyslexia's* connection to *dysgraphia* and *dyscalculia*?

Dyslexia is one of the three learning disorders listed by the APA (see p. 16), the other two being *dysgraphia* and *dyscalculia*. The Greek roots of the word *dysgraphia* have to do with impairment (*dys*) and writing letters (*graph*). People who have dysgraphia have a difficult time forming written letters, which can lead to challenges in writing in general. Occupational therapy is often part of the remedy for dysgraphia.

As for *dyscalculia*, which literally means "bad calculating," it is a mathematics impairment that affects a person's ability to understand numbers, do calculations, and engage in math problem solving. The Diagnostic and Statistical Manual-5 (DSM-5)—the encyclopedia therapists and psychiatrists in the United States are required to use to diagnose disorders—includes in its definition of dyscalculia: challenges with number sense, memorizing basic math facts, and quickly and accurately performing calculations (44).

Dyslexia can occur with other conditions, including other learning disorders, and it is certainly possible for a person with dyslexia to also have dysgraphia and/or dyscalculia.

Is dyslexia a visual problem? Do people who have dyslexia see things backwards? Do they see words backwards and letters reversed?

No, no, and no!

Perhaps one of the most common misconceptions about people who have dyslexia is that their dyslexia is *caused* by a visual problem and that they see words backwards or letters in reverse. Because dyslexia is neurobiological, it is involved with the body's vision system (eyes, optic nerve, visual cortex of the brain's occipital lobe). But for decades now, research has consistently shown that dyslexia is *not* caused by problems with vision and that people who have dyslexia do not see things backwards or view words and letters reversed (45, 46). For instance, in a well-known 1975 study, dyslexic and non-dyslexic English-speaking students were asked to reproduce a series of Hebrew letters that none of them had seen previously. The students with dyslexia were able to replicate individual letters and strings of letters just as accurately as the students who had no dyslexia (47).

Why, then, might a student reverse letters or write words backwards? Well, up to a certain age, it's normal for *any* child to reverse letters and numbers. And mirror writing (backwards writing) appears in the early stages of writing development among dyslexic and non-dyslexic children alike (48).

In his book, *Reading in the Brain: The New Science of How We Read*, neuroscientist Stanislas Dehaene explains that the brain tends to engage in mirror image generalization, a time saving trick that equates a flipped object with a non-flipped object (49). For example, imagine a sharpened pencil in front of you, its eraser on the left, and its graphite point on the right. If you flip the object horizontally, your brain instantly recognizes the "new" object, now with its point on the left and its eraser on the right. It's a pencil! There is no hesitation—your brain almost instantly says, "it's the same object, just mirrored."

But when is a flipped object absolutely *not* the same as its unflipped version? Reading teachers know it is when the object is a letter or a word. For example, this object—b—is the letter b. But when flipped, it's a totally different thing—now it's the letter d! The same goes for words like *was* and *pots*. When flipped, they are entirely new words—*saw* and *stop*. See Figure 1.2 for more mirror generalizations.

All of this is to say that many young children, dyslexic and non-dyslexic alike, tend to perceive flipped versions of a word to be the same as the non-flipped version, and vice versa, meaning it is not unusual for any kindergarten, first-grade, or even second-grade student to write *and* as *bna* or *cats* as *stac*. A young student's brain is simply equating one image with its mirror. Absolutely none of this has anything to do with seeing things backwards.

According to Dehaene, mirror image generalization of letters and words typically fades away by age seven or eight. Why? It's because dedicated teachers, often with the help of parents, repeatedly teach children the difference between a *d* and a *b* and show them that *bias* is not *said*,

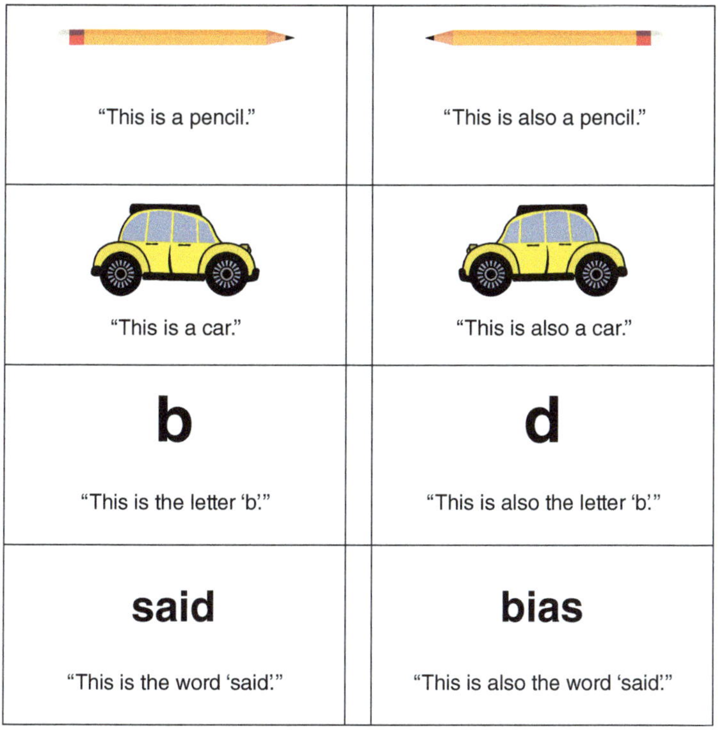

Figure 1.2 What Your Brain "Says" During Mirror Image Generalization

and vice versa. In effect, teachers train student brains to *stop* generalizing mirror images, at least when it comes to letters and words.

There is a caveat to all of this: some people do, in fact, have a great deal of left/right confusion, and this confusion can be a clue that reading problems are dyslexic in nature. If after persistent and effective handwriting instruction a child is still reversing many letters and writing many words backwards, and/or you notice a child is atypically confused about directionality (doesn't know left hand from right hand, confuses left and right during physical activities), you should take note.

What other common misconceptions exist about people with dyslexia?

With increased awareness and education, misconceptions about dyslexia are starting to die out or at least diminish in scope and intensity. Still, some false statements are hard to put to rest (remember loss aversion?). In the hope of replacing persistent myths, Figure 1.3 gives some definite truths.

Myth	*Truth*
Your ability to read is related to your intelligence. Therefore, if you don't read well, you must not be very smart.	Regarding dyslexia, there is absolutely no relation between the condition and IQ (50). People who experience dyslexia also experience a range of IQ levels, from high to typical. Thus, you can be intelligent *and* experience reading difficulties. As for the general relationship between IQ and reading ability, conditions such as a severe intellectual disability (of which low IQ is a part) will lead to difficulties in learning to read.
Reading is relatively easy and if a student is failing, it's because they are not working hard enough and spending enough time on homework. Students who aren't learning to read must be lazy. Teachers don't know what they are doing when it comes to teaching reading. Poor teaching is why struggling readers struggle.	Perhaps 50 percent or more of all children find it mildly to moderately difficult to learn how to read. Therefore, learning to read is not easy for many students (51). Research, including studies that make use of functional magnetic resonance imaging (*fMRI*) machines, consistently find evidence that people with dyslexia have inborn brain differences that make reading and spelling difficult (52). This difficulty with reading is not due to laziness, lack of effort, or poor teaching. Note: this is not to say people who have dyslexia sometimes don't work hard or that reading teachers are always effective. Rather, this is to say that the *origin* of dyslexia is not perceived laziness or poor teaching!
Dyslexia is incurable. If you start out as poor reader and speller, you will always be a poor reader and speller.	Dyslexia is not a disease and therefore it cannot be "cured." But its effects can be diminished and for many people, largely overcome. Early diagnosis is key, as is school support and the use of intensive, longitudinal, and systematic teaching practices. With everything in place, a student with dyslexia can not only experience general success in school but also become a much better reader, writer, and speller. Tens of thousands of teachers and students across the country know this truth.

Figure 1.3 Dyslexia Myths, Dyslexia Truths

Are people who have dyslexia exceptionally smart, talented, and creative? Does dyslexia provide people with an advantage of some type?

Some say yes and some say no.

It is comforting to think that dyslexia comes with a real upside, namely a high degree of intelligence and an ability to think in different ways that ultimately lead to creative accomplishments and/or business achievements. You may have heard of famous people with dyslexia: Henry Ford, Cher, Octavia Butler, Henry Winkler, Muhammad Ali, Whoopie Goldberg, Salma Hayek, and Pablo Picasso. These folks obviously have intellectual brilliance, exceptional skill sets, and/or remarkable creativity. And celebrities aside, I have several bright friends and acquaintances with dyslexia who excel at acting, teaching, writing books, and running a business.

Writer and entrepreneur Kate Griggs views dyslexia as an *ability*, one associated with many positive attributes, such as creativity, high degrees of relational and associational thinking, and a certain capacity to "see things differently" (53). For Griggs, dyslexia is a way of thinking that can lead to great innovation and discovery and is seen as a disability only within an educational setting. Researcher Maryanne Wolf expresses similar thoughts: "The brain organization that gives children with dyslexia significant advantages later in their lives – in areas such as art and architecture, pattern recognition in radiology and finance, and entrepreneurship – disadvantages them in their first years of learning" (54).

But other researchers caution against this type of thinking, emphatically stating that dyslexia is in no way a gift and that it confers *no* creative benefits (55). According to Dr. Louisa Moats, many people who have dyslexia are of normal intelligence and harbor no superior abilities in areas such as abstract reasoning or mechanical problem solving (56). Not to put too fine of a point on it but one possible rebuttal to the statistic that 40 percent of self-made millionaires have dyslexia (a statistic mentioned by Griggs and others) is that having dyslexia in a reading-based world may cause a person to develop the traits of hard work, resilience, and perseverance, all abilities that can help someone of typical talent and intelligence achieve great things. Putting your nose to the grindstone and never giving up are qualities that should never be underestimated.

Albert Einstein, a name synonymous with exceptional intelligence, is consistently and repeatedly highlighted as a person with dyslexia. But the Albert Einstein Archives say, "Einstein can certainly not be diagnosed with this [condition]" (57). And here's a final word from Dr. Louisa Moats: "Albert Einstein was *not* dyslexic."

Do scientists know all there is to know about dyslexia?

No. Research on dyslexia is ongoing and new avenues continue to be explored, including the role of executive functioning, why difficulties with rapid automatic naming arise, how difficulties with central auditory processing contribute to dyslexia, and what specific genes are implicated in the condition (58, 59). In the long run, efforts to understand are worthwhile because promise and solutions flow from understanding. Every day researchers are uncovering truths that may eventually translate into classroom actions that help students become better readers, writers, and spellers, especially those who struggle the most.

***

In this chapter, we learned that dyslexia is a complex condition that cannot be fully explained by any one theory or described by any single definition. The condition has many moving parts and researchers are still coming to an understanding of how they interact. Still, dyslexia *is* generally understandable, and anyone who works with children can and should have a strong foundation of knowledge about it.

Understanding dyslexia allows us to engage in classroom actions that help students become competent readers, writers, and spellers, and this is important. Although kids (and adults) are firmly in the throes of YouTube and TikTok, our current world—bursting with street signs, restaurant menus, and books like this one—is still very much a *reading* world, where information is passed along via text. For people to function within this world, they must be competent readers.

One piece of positive news is we can use our knowledge about dyslexia to help *all* students learn to read, write, and spell. To greater and lesser extents, what works for a child with dyslexia also works for a child without it! So, let's move to the next chapter, where we'll look at dyslexia from a classroom perspective, exploring student behaviors that can arise from dyslexia and considering co-occurring challenges that make learning to read especially difficult for some children.

End of Chapter Resources

1 Wolf, Maryanne, et al. 2024. "Towards a Dynamic, Comprehensive Conceptualization of Dyslexia." *Annals of Dyslexia* 74: 303–324. https://doi.org/10.1007/s11881-023-00297-1.

2 The Yale Center for Creativity & Dyslexia. 2024. "What is Dyslexia?" The Yale Center for Creativity & Dyslexia. http://dyslexia.yale.edu/dyslexia/what-is-dyslexia/.

3 International Dyslexia Association. 2002. "Definition of Dyslexia." International Dyslexia Association. https://dyslexiaida.org/definition-of-dyslexia/.

4 Wolf, Maryanne, et al. 2024. "Towards a Dynamic, Comprehensive Conceptualization of Dyslexia." *Annals of Dyslexia* 74: 303–324, p. 304. https://doi.org/10.1007/s11881-023-00297-1.

5 Wolf, Maryanne, et al. 2024. "Towards a Dynamic, Comprehensive Conceptualization of Dyslexia." *Annals of Dyslexia* 74: 303–324. https://doi.org/10.1007/s11881-023-00297-1.

6 University of Oxford. 2024. "A Brief History of Dyslexia." University of Oxford. https://dyslexiahistory.web.ox.ac.uk/brief-history-dyslexia.

7 Reading Rockets. 2024. "Profile: Guinevere Eden." Reading Rockets. www.readingrockets.org/people-and-organizations/guinevere-eden.

8 International Dyslexia Foundation Fact Sheet. 2015. "Dyslexia and the Brain." International Dyslexia Foundation. https://dyslexiaida.org/dyslexia-and-the-brain-fact-sheet/.

9 Wolf, Maryanne, et al. 2024. "Towards a Dynamic, Comprehensive Conceptualization of Dyslexia." *Annals of Dyslexia* 74: 303–324. https://doi.org/10.1007/s11881-023-00297-1.

10 Seidenberg, Mark. 2017. *Language at the Speed of Sight: How We Read, Why So Many Can't, and What We Can Do About It.* New York: Basic Books.

11 Glezer, Laurie, et al. 2015. "Adding Words to the Brain's Visual Dictionary: Novel Word Learning Selectively Sharpens Orthographic Representations in the VWFA." *Journal of Neuroscience* 35 (12): 4965–4972. https://doi.org/10.1523/JNEUROSCI.4031-14.2015.

12 Sutherland, Stephanie. 2015. "What Happens in the Brain When We Read?" *Scientific American Mind* 26 (4). doi:10.1038/scientificamericanmind0715-14.

13 Wolf, Maryanne, et al. 2024. "Towards a Dynamic, Comprehensive Conceptualization of Dyslexia." *Annals of Dyslexia* 74: 303–324. https://doi.org/10.1007/s11881-023-00297-1.

14 Wolf, Maryanne, and Patricia Grief Bowers. 1999. "The Double-Deficit Hypothesis for the Developmental Dyslexias." *Journal of Educational Psychology* 91 (3), 415–438.

15 Children of the Code. 2024. "Interview with Dr. Maryanne Wolf: Rapid Naming, Double-Deficits and Dyslexia." Children of the Code. https://childrenofthecode.org/interviews/wolf.htm.

16 Mark Seidenberg. 2024. "The Phonemic Awareness Discussion." Reading Matters. https://seidenbergreading.net/author/markseidenberg/.

17 Sonic Learning. 2019. "An Interview with Dr. Martha Burns: What is the Link Between CAPD and Dyslexia?" YouTube video, 1:09. www.youtube.com/watch?v=a1ZNqvqmRuY.

18 Shaywitz, Sally, and Jonathan Shaywitz. 2020. *Overcoming Dyslexia*. 2nd ed. New York: Alfred A. Knopf.

19 International Dyslexia Foundation Fact Sheet. 2020. *Dyslexia Basics*. International Dyslexia Foundation. https://dyslexiaida.org/dyslexia-and-the-brain-fact-sheet/.

20 American Psychiatric Association. 2024. "What is Specific Learning Disorder?" American Psychiatric Association. www.psychiatry.org/patients-families/specific-learning-disorder/what-is-specific-learning-disorder.

21 Dyslexia Help. 2024. "Debunking the Myths About Dyslexia." University of Michigan. https://dyslexiahelp.umich.edu/parents/learn-about-dyslexia/what-is-dyslexia/debunking-common-myths-about-dyslexia#:~:text=Myth%3A%20Intelligence%20and%20ability%20to,%2C%20middle%2C%20or%20low%20IQ's.

22 Wagner, Richard K., et al. 2020. "The Prevalence of Dyslexia: A New Approach to Its Estimation." *Journal of Learning Disabilities* 53 (5): 354–365. https://pmc.ncbi.nlm.nih.gov/articles/PMC8183124/.

23 Hu, Wei, et al. 2010. "Developmental Dyslexia in Chinese and English Populations: Dissociating the Effect of Dyslexia from Language Differences." National Institute of Health: National Library of Medicine. https://pubmed.ncbi.nlm.nih.gov/20488886/.

24 Ziegler, Johannes, et al. 2003. "Developmental Dyslexia in Different Languages: Language-Specific or Universal?" *Journal of Experimental Child Psychology* 86 (3): 169–193.
25 Ziegler, Johannes, et al. 2003. "Developmental Dyslexia in Different Languages: Language-Specific or Universal?" *Journal of Experimental Child Psychology* 86 (3): 169–193.
26 Sandman-Hurley, Kelli. 2024. "Dyslexia and the English Learner Dilemma." Language. www.languagemagazine.com/dyslexia-and-the-english-learner-dilemma/#:~:text=Fluency%20and%20orthography%20issues%20are,it%20is%20an%20opaque%20language.
27 TedXBrighton. 2017. "Kate Griggs: The Creative Brilliance of Dyslexia." YouTube video, 14:59. www.ted.com/talks/kate_griggs_the_creative_brilliance_of_dyslexia?subtitle=en.
28 Schumacher, Johannes, et al. 2007. "Genetics of Dyslexia: The Evolving Landscape." *Journal of Medical Genetics* 44 (5): 289–297, p. 289.
29 Dyslexia Research Trust. 2024. "Genetics of Dyslexia." Dyslexia Research Trust. www.dyslexic.org.uk/genetics-of-dyslexia.
30 Wolf, Maryanne, et al. 2024. "Towards a Dynamic, Comprehensive Conceptualization of Dyslexia." *Annals of Dyslexia* 74: 303–324. https://doi.org/10.1007/s11881-023-00297-1.
31 Psychology Today. 2018. "Are More Boys Than Girls Dyslexic? Does Sex Matter When It Comes To Dyslexia?" Psychology Today. www.psychologytoday.com/us/blog/raising-readers-writers-and-spellers/201404/are-more-boys-than-girls-dyslexic.
32 Shaywitz, Sally, et al. 1990. "Prevalence of Reading Disability in Boys and Girls. Results of the Connecticut Longitudinal Study." *Journal of the American Medical Association* 64 (8): 998–1002.
33 Shaywitz, Sally. 2003. *Overcoming Dyslexia: A New and Complete Science-Based Program for Reading Problems at Any Level.* New York: Alfred A. Knopf.
34 Dyslexia Help. 2024. "Debunking the Myths About Dyslexia." University of Michigan. https://dyslexiahelp.umich.edu/parents/learn-about-dyslexia/what-is-dyslexia/debunking-common-myths-about-dyslexia#:~:text=Myth%3A%20Intelligence%20and%20ability%20to,%2C%20middle%2C%20or%20low%20IQ's.
35 Rutter, Michael, et al. 2004. "Sex Differences in Developmental Reading Disability: New Findings from Four Epidemiology Studies." *Journal of the American Medical Association* 291 (16): 2007–2012.

36 Quinn, Jamie, and Richard Wagner. 2015. "Gender Differences in Reading Impairment and in the Identification of Impaired Readers: Results From a Large-Scale Study of At-Risk Readers." *Journal of Learning Disabilities* 48 (4): 433–445.

37 Quinn, Jamie, and Richard Wagner. 2015. "Gender Differences in Reading Impairment and in the Identification of Impaired Readers: Results From a Large-Scale Study of At-Risk Readers." *Journal of Learning Disabilities* 48 (4): 433–445.

38 Sonic Learning. 2019. "An Interview with Dr. Martha Burns: Is Dyslexia More Common in Males?" YouTube video, 0:52. www.youtube.com/watch?v=sDwcUJsxaHk.

39 Arnett, Anne, et al. 2017. "Explaining the Sex Difference in Dyslexia." *Journal of Child Psychology and Psychiatry* 58 (6): 719–727.

40 Reading Rockets. 2024. "Profile: Guinevere Eden." Reading Rockets. www.readingrockets.org/people-and-organizations/guinevere-eden.

41 Yoncheva, Yulia, Jessica Wise, and Bruce McCandliss. 2015. "Hemispheric Specialization for Visual Words is Shaped by Attention to Sublexical Units During Initial Learning." *Brain and Language* 145–146: 23–33.

42 American Psychiatric Association. 2024. "What is Specific Learning Disorder?" American Psychiatric Association. www.psychiatry.org/patients-families/specific-learning-disorder/what-is-specific-learning-disorder.

43 American Psychiatric Association. 2024. "What is Specific Learning Disorder?" American Psychiatric Association. www.psychiatry.org/patients-families/specific-learning-disorder/what-is-specific-learning-disorder.

44 Petretto, Donatella, and Carmelo Masala. 2017. "Dyslexia and Specific Learning Disorders: New International Diagnostic Criteria." *Journal of Childhood and Developmental Disorders* 3 (4): 9.

45 International Literacy Association. 2016. "Research Advisory: Dyslexia." International Literacy Association. http://readingrecovery.org/wp-content/uploads/2016/12/ila-dyslexia-research-advisory_2016.pdf.

46 Vellutino, Frank, Jack Fletcher, Margaret Snowling, et al. 2004. "Specific Reading Disability (Dyslexia): What Have We Learned in the Past Four Decades?" *Journal of Child Psychology and Psychiatry* 45 (1): 2–40.

47 Vellutino, Frank, et al. 1975. "Visual Form Perception in Deficient and Normal Readers as a Function of Age and Orthographic-Linguistic Familiarity." *Cortex* 11: 22–30.

48 Dehaene, Stanislas. 2009. *Reading in the Brain: The New Science of How We Read.* New York: Penguin (Random House).

49 Dehaene, Stanislas. 2009. *Reading in the Brain: The New Science of How We Read.* New York: Penguin (Random House).

50 Iowa Reading Research Center. 2023. "The Neuroscience of Reading With Dr. G. Reid Lyon." Iowa Reading Research Center. https://irrc.education.uiowa.edu/blog/2023/05/neuroscience-reading-dr-g-reid-lyon.

51 Dyslexia Help. 2024. "Debunking the Myths About Dyslexia." University of Michigan. https://dyslexiahelp.umich.edu/parents/learn-about-dyslexia/what-is-dyslexia/debunking-common-myths-about-dyslexia#:~:text=Myth%3A%20Intelligence%20and%20ability%20to,%2C%20middle%2C%20or%20low%20IQ's.

52 International Dyslexia Foundation Fact Sheet. 2015. "Dyslexia and the Brain." International Dyslexia Foundation. https://dyslexiaida.org/dyslexia-and-the-brain-fact-sheet/.

53 TedXBrighton. 2017. "Kate Griggs: The Creative Brilliance of Dyslexia." YouTube video, 14:59. www.ted.com/talks/kate_griggs_the_creative_brilliance_of_dyslexia?subtitle=en

54 Wolf, Maryanne. 2018. *Reader Come Home: The Reading Brain in the Digital Age.* New York: Harper Collins.

55 Erbeli, Florina, Peng Peng, and Marianne Rice. 2022. "No Evidence of Creative Benefit Accompanying Dyslexia: A Meta-Analysis." *Journal of Learning Disabilities* 55 (3): 242–253.

56 International Dyslexia Association. 2024. "Dr. Lousia Moats Debunks Five Popular Myths About Dyslexia." International Dyslexia Association. https://dyslexiaida.org/louisa-moats-debunks-five-popular-myths-about-dyslexia/.

57 Albert Einstein Archives. 2025. "The Legend of the Dull-Witted Child Who Grew Up to Be a Genius." Albert Einstein Archives. www.albert-einstein.org/article_handicap.html.

58 Carnegie Learning. 2024. "Research Updates." Carnegie Learning. www.carnegielearning.com/blog/2023-dyslexia-research-updates/.

59 The Dyslexia Foundation. 2024. "New Research" The Dyslexia Foundation. https://dyslexiafoundation.org/category/newresearch/.

CHAPTER **2**

Dyslexia in the Classroom

The negative effects of dyslexia can be mitigated, a little to a lot, when a student is given appropriate instruction as early as possible. One thing is for sure: without effective teaching, reading difficulties only grow worse. Sadly, some students are not identified as dyslexic until they reach the upper grades or adulthood, if at all. This sets them back, certainly in reading achievement and often in areas of mental health and social functioning. Students who experience years of reading difficulties are more likely to suffer anxiety and depression, lack confidence and self-esteem, drop out of school, and become incarcerated (1). The good news is that reading difficulties, including those that are dyslexic in nature, can be overcome and even prevented, and feelings of stress and frustration can be greatly lessened when school systems are staffed with knowledgeable teachers capable of recognizing the signs of dyslexia, implementing effective instructional practices, and providing supports.

In this chapter we will examine how dyslexia differs from other reading difficulties, emphasizing observable classroom behaviors that enable us to confidently say, "This student may have dyslexia." Confidence rooted in knowledge empowers us to take action, such as teaching in ways that truly help students master reading and spelling, as well as starting an evaluation process that can formally rule dyslexia in or out.

What language and literacy behaviors might indicate dyslexia?

Generally speaking, students with dyslexia exhibit a surprising or unexpected difficulty in learning to read. Specifically, this difficulty takes the form of any or all of the following:

- Difficulty mastering sound–letter associations.
- Poor decoding skills.
- Inaccurate word reading.
- Accurate but slow word reading.
- Difficulty mastering grammar concepts.
- Chronically poor spelling, on tests and/or within authentic writing.
- Difficulty finding the right word while speaking; unexpected pauses during speech.
- Difficulty learning phonological skills, such as generating words that rhyme or segmenting a word into discrete sounds (2).

Please note that each of these bulleted difficulties can happen in a variety of combinations and intensities. As a student exhibits more behaviors that have greater intensity, teachers may increasingly wonder if the reading problem is dyslexic in nature.

Why are these behaviors dyslexic in nature? Don't most children have a difficult time with reading?

First, let's get a sense of how easily all children learn to read (3, 4, 5). Perhaps 10 percent of children in America learn to read relatively quickly and easily. Their progress seems effortless and their grandparents think they are geniuses! Another 30–40 percent reach reading proficiency with a typical amount of effective, broad instruction. Finally, 50–60 percent of all children have a challenging time learning to read, write, and spell. This in no way means they are destined to experience a full-blown reading difficulty. But it does means that, to master foundational literacy skills, they will need to receive considerable amounts of effective instruction, such as direct and explicit teaching in phonics and spelling, decodable text, extra repetition, lots of practice reading authentic texts, and explicit instruction and practice in comprehension strategies.

Theoretically, when taught with effective best practices, the bulk of students for whom learning to read is difficult will follow a typical trajectory of achievement, repeatedly making a year's worth of progress in general education classrooms and needing no, or perhaps very little, tutoring or specialized intervention. There is a subset of students, though, perhaps 5–15 percent, who might make slower progress toward mastering fundamental reading skills, even when powerful instruction is given repeatedly and consistently. These children may have dyslexia.

What other signs or traits suggest a student may have dyslexia?

It's helpful to think of dyslexia as a profile of traits and characteristics. Some manifest during reading, writing, and spelling tasks. Others do not. As signs or clues start to accumulate, you might increasingly suspect that a student's reading difficulty is due to dyslexia. These additional signs may include:

- a family member who has dyslexia or a serious reading problem,
- a general degree of intelligence that gives you reason to think the student should be easily learning to read,
- difficulty with rapidly identifying objects, colors, and/or letters,
- trouble with directions, that is, not easily knowing left from right,
- difficulty in learning a second language,
- a creative thinker and/or a thinker with good background knowledge and an ability to see connections,
- difficulty attending to a variety of tasks.

How can I tell if a kindergartener or first grader might have dyslexia?

In kindergarten and first grade, students are just beginning to develop reading, writing, and spelling skills. This means they will exhibit numerous errors and confusions. Still, the signs of dyslexia can appear as early as preschool (6) and as you carefully observe young students in action and assess their progress in reading and spelling, some skill deficits and behaviors will stand out. If certain aspects of literacy development are notably problematic (determined through observation and assessments), and if you have ruled out other causes of reading difficulties (for example, missing a lot of school, being chronically tired, etc.), then you might suspect dyslexia.

Signs to look for in kindergarten and first-grade children include:

- chronic complaining about how hard reading is,
- trying to avoid reading tasks by crying, not volunteering, refusing to engage,
- regularly failing to associate letters with sounds; reading errors that show no connection to the sounds of letters on the page,
- failing to sound out even simple words like *fit*, *sum*, *get*,
- showing a bright and curious affect but making minimal progress in learning how to read,
- having great trouble with directions; not easily learning left from right,
- having difficulty finding the right word while speaking; showing unexpected pauses during speech,
- on assessments, cannot rapidly name objects, colors, and/or letters.

Are attention deficit disorder (ADD) and attention deficit with hyperactivity disorder (ADHD) associated with dyslexia?

Yes.

There are many reasons a child might fidget, not attend to a task, and find learning to read difficult. Reasons for these types of behaviors may have less to do with ADHD and dyslexia and more to do with a lack of sleep, a cultural difference, or a task that isn't suited to the developmental level of the child. On the other hand, we know that ADHD and ADD are real conditions and that a certain number of children have them. We also know ADD/ADHD is associated with dyslexia. For example, researchers examining the prevalence of co-occurring factors that cause reading difficulties estimate that between 25 and 40 percent of students with dyslexia have ADHD (7) and about 25–35 percent of students characterized with ADHD/ADD have dyslexia (8). Either way you look at it, it's not that unusual for a student to have both dyslexia and ADHD. But this doesn't mean that one causes the other. It's just that they often show up together, and scientists continue to look into why this might be (9, 10).

In a classroom setting, what are the best predictors of dyslexia?

As a teacher of reading, it is helpful to know of any observable deficits that more definitively point to dyslexia. So, the question becomes: Are there specific skills that when in deficit, strongly predict that a reading difficulty is due to dyslexia? The answer to this question is yes. And two seem most pressing.

According to multiple studies done over many years, the two best predictors of dyslexia across most languages are 1) a deficit in phonological awareness skills, and 2) a deficit in rapid automatic naming, which is a proxy for reading fluency (11). Thus, phonological awareness (especially phonemic awareness) and rapid automatic naming are two areas to closely monitor, especially in young students. In the next chapter, we will discuss screeners and formative assessments that can give teachers and instructional support systems information for both areas.

Pay special attention to how your students perform during phonemic deletion and substitution tasks (12). An example of a deletion task is this: "Say the word jam. [Student says/jam/.] Now say it without the/j/. [Students says, /am/.] An example of a substitution task is this: "Say the word sit. [Student says /sit/.] Now say it with the /a/ sound. [Students says, /sat/.] Read more about these type of tasks and the researcher who suggests using them in Chapter 3.

If a student has deficits in phonological awareness, rapid automatic naming, or both, it in no way means the student definitely has dyslexia. But there is a robust body of evidence that shows children who are deficit in both areas are much more likely to have developmental dyslexia (13, 14, 15).

As a reminder, the two deficit areas correspond to two of the three eternal triangle areas (see Figure 1.1), namely the orthographic and phonological. We know that these two areas affect each other as reading develops (16) and so can see how deficits in each might lead to a condition like dyslexia.

Based on what we've learned, one way to *begin* to define dyslexia is to say that it's an unexpected difficulty in learning to read brought about by neurobiological differences in the brain's reading circuit, especially in the phonological and orthographic processing areas.

How can I tell if a multi-language learner has dyslexia?

Dyslexia is a biological condition, not a cultural one, arising from brain differences that cause reading and spelling difficulties for anyone attempting to decode and encode a printed alphabetic language. Therefore, dyslexia exists in a subset of people around the world, regardless of their native language (17).

Identifying dyslexia is a tricky business and, in this book, we are talking about first language English speakers. When it comes to struggling multi-language learners, the task is even more complicated because an assessor has to separate a reading difficulty rooted in a language issue from a reading difficulty caused by dyslexia. Remember, the two can co-occur. Still, many trained evaluators can determine if multi-language learners are dyslexic or not. To do so, they must pay attention to the skills that best predict dyslexia, observe students as they use their native tongue, and assess them in their native language (18).

For teachers working with multi-language learners, it is suggested that you monitor the areas bulleted next (19). If any or all are problematic, you might suspect dyslexia:

- Phonemic awareness ability in the student's native language.
- Rapid automatic naming of visually presented objects, letters, and/or numbers.
- Reading fluency (a proxy for rapid automatic naming) in the student's native language.
- Spelling ability (orthography) in the student's native language.
- The family's history of reading success or difficulty.

Can ineffective teaching practices cause reading difficulties that mimic dyslexia?

Absolutely!

Teaching is a noble profession, full of caring people, many of whom are effective teachers. But unfortunately, some teachers lack an awareness of effective practices and this causes or exacerbates reading difficulties. The reasons for ineffective teaching vary. Some teachers are underprepared or undertrained. Some don't receive adequate professional development. And some have difficulty moving from their traditional methods to the most informed, effective practices. Also, high rates of teacher turnover can contribute to low reading scores in a school.

Ineffective teaching, which includes not teaching essential areas (like decoding skills) to mastery, leads to a weak foundation of reading and spelling, especially if the ineffective teaching occurs in consecutive primary grades. In turn, a weak foundation can impact a reader for years to come. The symptoms that arise from ineffective teaching often *mimic* dyslexia and include inaccurate spelling, a lack of decoding skills, guessing at words, low fluency rates, and weak comprehension.

The obvious remedy to this issue is effective teaching and a robust support system!

Can students' compensatory behaviors cause a teacher to think they don't have dyslexia?

Yes, at least for a time.

Students can mask reading and spelling deficits, engaging in "work arounds" that can mislead unsuspecting parents and teachers for months and even years. This is especially true if the child is bright. Clever kids can come up with compensatory strategies that mask their lack of foundational skills. These offsetting skills can include memorizing, using context, having friends assist in some way, using background knowledge, using skills of association and relation to make fairly accurate guesses, being extra hard working, pleasing the teacher with good behavior, or even subtly borrowing from their peers' work.

Also, traits of dyslexia sometimes appear in surprising combinations that might cause a teacher to say, "That's not dyslexia." For example, it is possible for a second-grade student to consistently ace spelling tests, use a wide vocabulary, have a strong ability to pay attention, do well in math, and also exhibit relatively weak reading skills. Because many aspects of the student's school performance are strong, a teacher might not give enough weight to the poor reading. If no one raises a red flag on this child until the third or fourth grade, valuable years of remediation will be lost.

Does a lack of progress in an intervention group indicate dyslexia?

Perhaps.

In the face of a strong intervention program, a lack of appropriate progress can be a clue that a student has dyslexia. For example, imagine a reading interventionist who is working with four low-achieving second graders using a program such as *Really Great Reading*, Lindamood-Bell's *Seeing Stars*, or Wilson's *Fundations*. After sixteen weeks of instruction, two of the children are achieving appropriate rates of growth and are approaching typical second-grade benchmarks. But two students are showing minimal growth, which is surprising because they are bright, hardworking, and engaged. When added to other signs and assessment data points, this lack of growth during an intervention could make a teacher think the students have dyslexia.

On the other hand, some children fail to make appropriate progress in an intervention program for reasons other than dyslexia. Maybe the program isn't crafted in a way that engages the reader's interest and efforts, or perhaps it has so many rules and routines for encoding and decoding words that it confuses a student. Maybe the student is preoccupied with difficulties at home or perhaps the child has developed an undiagnosed vision or hearing problem. None of these issues, all which can impact reading achievement, are dyslexic in nature.

What non-literacy classroom behaviors might arise if a student has dyslexia?

Problematic behaviors often arise from reading difficulties, whether or not they originate in dyslexia. So, let's consider these behaviors for a moment.

In my graduate school days, I learned a child's negative classroom behaviors always serve a function. At the root of every behavior—be it crying, silliness, yelling, or bolting from the classroom—is a behavioral goal: to gain attention, to gain power and control, to avoid or escape a task, to gain sensory stimulation (20).

As with all human beings, children who have dyslexia respond to challenging and frustrating tasks in myriad ways. Some dig in and try to persevere. Others try to avoid or escape the situation, meaning they work really hard to *not* read, write, and spell! During literacy instruction, be on the lookout for avoidance and escape behaviors such as:

- quietness and passivity, trying to avoid being called on,
- complaining that reading is too hard or too boring,
- crying,
- silliness,
- refusal to work,
- angry outbursts,
- undue confidence and/or braggadocio.

In addition, try to compare literacy-time behaviors with behaviors that occur in other settings. Do the avoidance behaviors also happen in math class and gym class or during chorus? If yes, something other than dyslexia could be causing the behaviors.

Here's a final thought: keep your eyes on the bright worker bees who sometimes make surprising mistakes during reading and spelling. Some children have a great capacity to power through tasks that are difficult, and, as mentioned earlier, they may be bright enough to develop strategies that mask their lack of foundational skills. With a pleasing demeanor and a B grade in language arts (which really doesn't tell us anything, does it?), these students can make it all the way to fourth or fifth grade before someone suspects they have dyslexia.

Can dyslexia be outgrown?

No. But its effects can be diminished, sometimes greatly (21).

The idea that dyslexia can be "outgrown" is a myth (22). Likewise, it's a mistake for a parent or teacher to *wait* to address reading difficulties, assuming they will fade with time. Dyslexia is a lifelong issue because it arises from differences in brain circuitry. When a person has dyslexia, their difficulties with phonological processing, rapid automatic naming, "word finding" during reading and possibly speaking, and/or accurate spelling will persist throughout their life.

This is not to say dyslexia can't be managed or remediated. It can. As soon as a child begins to exhibit a reading difficulty, teachers (and parents) should take actions that plan for, support, and teach that student.

This is true whether the difficulty is caused by dyslexia or not. Early and effective intervention helps students lessen their deficit literacy skills and even overcome them, to greater and lesser extents. Other issues that sometimes arise from dyslexia can be overcome, too, including anxiety, frustration, low self-esteem, and difficulty with concentration.

Does the term dyslexia describe a mild, moderate, or severe reading difficulty?

Dyslexia exists on a spectrum. The Michigan Dyslexia Help website says "Some people may have more mild forms [of dyslexia], while others may experience it more severely" (23). Meanwhile, the American Psychiatric Association says learning disorders such as dyslexia can vary in severity (meaning they exist as a continuum), describing the range with the terms mild, moderate, and severe (24).

For me, a defining feature of dyslexia is that a person with it regularly experiences significant disruptions in the reading-based world. Learning to read is hard, sometimes very hard, and so is the act of reading. Similarly, the more severe forms of dyslexia can involve significant deficits in oral language and rapid naming of letters and objects, all of which require more intensive intervention (25).

What conditions other than dyslexia might cause reading difficulties?

Reading difficulties arise for many reasons. Consider the eternal triangle [Figure 1.1], with its three areas wired for reading: semantic (meaning), phonological (sound), and orthographic (spelling). Now consider a student who lacks understanding of text. The possible reasons for a semantic difficulty are numerous: the student might have an underlying physiological issue, such as an intellectual disability caused by lead exposure or Down's Syndrome, they might lack background knowledge due to socio-economic issues, they might not have vocabulary because they don't read widely (and spend too much time on screens), perhaps English is not their native language.

Sometimes students experience reading difficulties due to deficits in foundational reading skills; their lack of these bedrock skills could be because they missed instruction, experienced homelessness, suffered a protracted illness, or even lived through a world-wide pandemic! And as mentioned before, ineffective teaching methods, a lack of appropriate instruction, and/or a weak instructional support system in a school can all cause or exacerbate a reading difficulty.

Finally, when compared to other WEIRD countries (western, educated, industrialized, rich, and democratic), America has a unique set of social and cultural factors that make educating kids difficult. Our country's wide income inequality, relatively weak social safety net, high rates of childhood poverty, and lingering systemic racism all contribute to the chance that a child will develop a reading problem.

Any or all of these conditions, from exposure to lead to missed reading instruction, can interact in varying ways to cause reading, writing, and spelling difficulties that look like the deficits caused by dyslexia. So, one has stay alert to all the possibilities and give time to observation, assessment, and applying professional knowledge. Only then can a teacher gain a clearer sense of why a student might be struggling.

Students with dyslexia typically lack text comprehension because they have difficulties decoding text and finding words in their orthographic processing area (26). Slow and/or inaccurate word reading diminishes comprehension, limits the amount of text that can be read (thereby constraining acquisition of vocabulary and background knowledge), and frustrates the reader, causing them to not want to read. The end result is a kind of negative feedback loop: a lack of reading diminishes background knowledge and vocabulary, which further diminishes understanding of text, which makes reading more difficult, which makes a student want to avoid reading… you get the idea.

***

In this chapter, we discussed observing our classroom students with an eye toward dyslexia, asking if the behaviors they exhibit are signs of the condition. When we see a student continuing to struggle in the face of effective instruction, have ruled-out non-dyslexic causes of reading difficulties, and observed additional clues, such as a family history of reading difficulties, then we might suspect dyslexia. As we continue to give effective instruction, our next move will be to alert the parents and the school team that the student might need to be considered for a formal assessment.

In the next chapter, we'll explore the evaluation process that determines if a student has dyslexia, a process that includes observation, screening, gathering data and information from parents and other teachers, and a formal evaluation given by a professional assessor. We'll also look at measures that assess dyslexia, from classroom screeners to the tests an experienced diagnostician might use.

End of Chapter Resources

1 McArthur, Genevieve, and Anne Castles. 2017. "Helping Children with Reading Difficulties: Some Things We Have Learned So Far." *npj Science of Learning* 2 (7). https://doi.org/10.1038/s41539-017-0008-3.

2 International Dyslexia Association. 2017. *Dyslexia in the Classroom: What Every Teacher Needs to Know*. International Dyslexia Association. https://dyslexiaida.org/wp-content/uploads/2015/01/DITC-Handbook.pdf.

3 Lyon, Reid. 1998. "Why Reading Is Not a Natural Process." *Educational Leadership* 55 (6): 14–18.

4 National Institute of Child Health and Human Development, NIH, DHHS. 2000. *National Reading Panel: Teaching Children to Read: An Evidence-Based Assessment of the Scientific Research Literature on Reading and Its Implications for Reading Instruction: Reports of the Subgroups*. Washington, DC: U.S. Government Printing Office. Also available online at www.nichd.nih.gov/sites/default/files/publications/pubs/nrp/Documents/report.pdf.

5 Young, Nancy, and Jan Hasbrouck. 2024. *Climbing the Ladder of Reading and Writing: Meeting the Needs of ALL Learners*. Infographic, xvi. New York: Benchmark Education.

6 International Dyslexia Association. 2024. "It's a Myth That Young Children Cannot Be Screened for Dyslexia." International Dyslexia Association. https://dyslexiaida.org/its-a-myth-that-young-children-cannot-be-screened-for-dyslexia/.

7 McGrath, Lauren, and Catherine Stoodley. 2019. "Are There Shared Neural Correlates Between Dyslexia and ADHD? A Meta-Analysis of Voxel-based Morphometry Studies." *Journal of Neurodevelopmental Disorders* 11 (31). https://doi.org/10.1186/s11689-019-9287-8.

8 Fletcher, Jack, and Elena Grigorenko. 2017. "Neuropsychology of Learning Disabilities: The Past and the Future." *Journal of the International Neuropsychological Society* 23 (9–10): 930–940.

9 Germanò, Eva, Antonella Gagliano, and Paolo Curatolo. 2010. "Comorbidity of ADHD and Dyslexia." *Developmental Neuropsychology* 35 (5): 475–493.

10 Lonergan, Aoife, et al. 2019. "A Meta-Analysis of Executive Functioning in Dyslexia With Consideration of the Impact of Comorbid ADHD." *Journal of Cognitive Psychology* 31 (7): 725–749.

11 Ozernov-Palchik Ola, et al. 2017. "Longitudinal Stability of Pre-Reading Skill Profiles of Kindergarten Children: Implications For Early Screening and Theories of Reading." *Developmental Science* 20 (5): 10.

12 Kilpatrick, David. 2015. *The Essentials of Assessing, Preventing, and Overcoming Reading Difficulties*. Hoboken, NJ: Wiley & Sons, p. 179.

13 Norton, Elizabeth, et al. 2014. "Functional Neuroanatomical Evidence for the Double-Deficit Hypothesis for Developmental Dyslexia." *Neuropsychologia* 61: 235–246. https://doi.org/10.1016/j.neuropsychologia.2014.06.015.

14 Wolf, Maryanne, et al. 2024. "Towards a Dynamic, Comprehensive Conceptualization of Dyslexia." *Annals of Dyslexia* 74: 303–324. https://doi.org/10.1007/s11881-023-00297-1.

15 Wolf, Maryanne, and Patricia Bowers. 2000. "Naming-Speed Processes and Developmental Reading Disabilities: An Introduction to the Special Issue on the Double-Deficit Hypothesis." *Journal of Learning Disabilities* 33 (4): 322–324. https://doi.org/10.1177/002221940003300404.

16 Seidenberg, Mark. 2024. "The Phonemic Awareness Discussion." Reading Matters. https://seidenbergreading.net/author/markseidenberg/.

17 Sandman-Hurley, Kelli. 2024. "Dyslexia and the English Learner Dilemma." Language. www.languagemagazine.com/dyslexia-and-the-english-learner-dilemma/#:~:text=Fluency%20and%20orthography%20issues%20are,it%20is%20an%20opaque%20language.

18 Sandman-Hurley, Kelli. 2024. "Dyslexia and the English Learner Dilemma." Language. www.languagemagazine.com/dyslexia-and-the-english-learner-dilemma/#:~:text=Fluency%20and%20orthography%20issues%20are,it%20is%20an%20opaque%20language.

19 Rodrigo, Mercedes, et al. 2004. "Assessment of Orthographical Processing in Spanish Children with Dyslexia: The Role of Lexical and Sublexical Units." *Electronic Journal of Research in Educational Psychology* 2 (4).

20 How To ABA. 2004. "Understanding the Functions of Behavior in ABA." How To ABA. https://howtoaba.com/functions-of-behaviour/.
21 International Dyslexia Association. 2023. "Dyslexia At a Glance." International Dyslexia Association. https://dyslexiaida.org/dyslexia-at-a-glance/.
22 Dyslexia Help. 2024. "Debunking the Myths About Dyslexia." University of Michigan. https://dyslexiahelp.umich.edu/parents/learn-about-dyslexia/what-is-dyslexia/debunking-common-myths-about-dyslexia#:~:text=Myth%3A%20Intelligence%20and%20ability%20to,%2C%20middle%2C%20or%20low%20IQ's.
23 Dyslexia Help. 2024. "Debunking the Myths About Dyslexia." University of Michigan. https://dyslexiahelp.umich.edu/parents/learn-about-dyslexia/what-is-dyslexia/debunking-common-myths-about-dyslexia#:~:text=Myth%3A%20Intelligence%20and%20ability%20to,%2C%20middle%2C%20or%20low%20IQ's.
24 American Psychiatric Association. 2024. "What is Specific Learning Disorder?" American Psychiatric Association. www.psychiatry.org/patients-families/specific-learning-disorder/what-is-specific-learning-disorder
25 Snowling, Margaret, et al. 2020. "Dyslexia and Developmental Language Disorder: Comorbid Disorders With Distinct Effects on Reading Comprehension." *Journal of Child Psychology and Psychiatry* 61 (6): 672–680.
26 Stevens, Elizabeth, Colby Hall, and Sharon Vaughn. 2022. "Language and Reading Comprehension For Students With Dyslexia: An Introduction to the Special Issue." *The Annals of Dyslexia* 72: 197–203. https://doi.org/10.1007/s11881-022-00260-6.

CHAPTER 3

Evaluation and Diagnosis

When a student unexpectedly and consistently has a difficult time learning to read, at some point a teacher might say, "This child should be tested for dyslexia." But *tested* isn't quite the right word. As the International Dyslexia Association (IDA) points out, a more appropriate word is *evaluated*. To quote the IDA, the term *evaluation* describes:

> … the process of determining if someone has dyslexia. [It] encompasses identification, screening, testing, diagnosis, and all the other information gathering involved when the student, their family, and a team of professionals work together to determine why the student is having difficulty and what can be done to help (1).

Determining dyslexia is a complex endeavor, requiring input from teachers, parents, and certainly assessment experts. Because the condition is best understood as a collection of traits that arise from nature (genetics and neurobiology) and are influenced by nurture (from culture to socioeconomics), teachers will be asked to collect evaluation information from a variety of sources and in a number of ways. These include classroom behavior checklists, notes from parent–teacher conferences, and numerous literacy-related pieces of work and assessments, such as writing samples, spelling tests, and oral reading fluency probes. Simultaneously, teachers must decide how to best teach the student as the evaluation process unfolds over time.

In this chapter, we'll examine the roles classroom teachers play in a dyslexia evaluation. Regardless of the outcome, the process gives a classroom teacher valuable details on the strengths and weaknesses of a student and points the way to effective instruction that can help the child overcome their reading difficulties.

What is a teacher's role in the assessment and diagnosis of dyslexia?

Let's start with these two thoughts:

1. Because an evaluation process is shaped by state laws, district mandates, and the support of parents and teachers, any process for assessing and diagnosing dyslexia will vary (sometimes greatly) between schools and school districts.
2. Teachers do not diagnose dyslexia.

Regarding number two, only a trained diagnostician using a battery of psychological and educational assessments can definitively determine if a student has dyslexia. Still, based on a student's classroom behaviors, family history, and assessment information (from formative and benchmark assessments to progress monitoring probes and screening scores), classroom teachers can certainly suspect the condition—and possibly strongly. A powerful suspicion should lead to two things: classroom teaching designed to give that student the foundational literacy skills they need, and steps toward a formal evaluation.

What are the steps of a dyslexia evaluation process?

The steps and sequences for an evaluation can vary from state to state and district to district. Thus, the following list includes a common ordering of the evaluation process, but may not align directly with the requirements of your school or district (2, 3).

- The teacher becomes educated about what dyslexia is and understands the spectrum of traits, characteristics, and signs that suggest it.
- The teacher observes and assesses all students while teaching. Formative assessments generate reading, spelling, and writing scores. Observation leads to notes about reading difficulties and the factors that might be causing them, from being a multi-language learner to a lack of repetition in a particular skill or insufficient instruction in previous years.
- Teachers, interventionists, and/or school psychologists give a dyslexia screener or screeners, either to every student or to a subset of students. Classroom teachers use the scores to guide instruction. The scores from the assessments are seen and discussed by others, such as the school psychologists, reading interventionists, and the school principal, all of whom sit on some version of a student support team.
- Using effective teaching practices, the teacher teaches students who are having reading difficulties (see Chapter 5). In addition, the classroom teacher gives struggling students a specific reading intervention or interventions, most likely in a small group. Also, the student might go to a reading interventionist in a separate setting. Interventions inside and outside the general education classroom generate assessment data.
- In some instances, the classroom teacher notes additional signs that might suggest dyslexia, such as a family history of reading difficulties, a lack of progress in initiated interventions, a personality profile that should lead to reading acquisition (the student is smart, has background knowledge, likes school) but isn't, and non-literacy behaviors sometimes associated with dyslexia (task avoidance, fidgeting and inattention, thinking in creative ways).
- Based on the screening scores, observational notes, and assessment data, the teacher in conjunction with a school team suggests to parents that the student undergo a formal dyslexia assessment given by a trained evaluator.

Can classroom teachers play a part in screening students for dyslexia?

Absolutely. But training is necessary.

If possible, classroom teachers should take part in administering screeners. After all, they know their students best. And some students perform better on an assessment when a familiar teacher is the one giving it. Additionally, screeners give classroom teachers real-time information they can use to guide their instruction.

Giving a screener is, of course, dependent upon a teacher having been trained on how to give it. Another necessity is time, as in having time to screen students, analyze the results (typically done in collaboration with an assessment team), and plan for instruction based on the scores.

Is it possible to screen young children for dyslexia?

Yes.

Surprisingly, the misinformed idea that a student cannot be referred for a dyslexia evaluation before second grade is still alive and well in some education systems. In fact, it is possible to evaluate young children and identify potential reading difficulties well before problems turn into reading failures and frustrations (4). Beginning in kindergarten and possibly earlier, screeners can be given to all children in a school's primary grades. Here the goal is to locate students who are "at risk" for a reading difficulty, provide appropriate instruction, and monitor progress.

In an article for the IDA, researcher Dr. Nadine Gaab says, "It's a myth that young children cannot be screened for dyslexia!" (5). While debunking this big myth, she also fact checks several other inaccuracies.

Myth	*Truth*
Signs of dyslexia can be seen only after two to three years of reading instruction.	It's true that a final diagnosis of dyslexia requires a student to experience significant reading difficulties. But it's also true that early signs of dyslexia can be observed at a preschool age and possibly earlier. Deficits in phonological awareness, rapid automatic naming, verbal working memory, and letter knowledge strongly predict dyslexia in children as young as age three (6, 7).
Early intervention is not effective.	Early intervention is most certainly effective! Research studies point to the importance of effective classroom reading instruction in the early grades and early interventions for at-risk students. These actions improve reading achievement in the current classroom setting, as well as the effectiveness of future remediation should it become necessary (8).

(Continued)

Early screening costs too much for school districts.	Early screening doesn't have to be costly. Some assessments used for screening, like Kilpatrick's PAST and the Acadience RAN, are free! Additionally, many districts assess older, low-achieving students with tools that also work as early screeners, and special education teachers and reading interventionists are already trained to use them. Finally, putting money toward preventing reading difficulties is less costly than remediating difficulties once they occur.

Is early identification of dyslexia important?

Yes!

Early identification and intervention are critically important for better outcomes later (9). Some children with dyslexia who get appropriate instruction in kindergarten and first grade improve their reading skills enough to be successful in grade school and then high school (10). Amazingly, the human brain's plasticity not only enables it to surmount strokes and recover from traumas, but it also allows for re-wiring in a way that lessens reading difficulties. This surprising malleability of the brain is great news for students who have dyslexia, especially if proper instruction is given early in a child's schooling.

Waiting to give the right kinds of instruction only makes teaching and learning more difficult. For example, because dyslexia is neurobiological in nature and brain plasticity decreases as childhood unfolds, late kindergarten interventions bring about progress much more quickly than fourth-grade reading interventions (11). Also, the amount of remedial content a student is expected to cover steadily increases with the grades, making it challenging for older students to simultaneously become better readers and meet curricular expectations. Therefore, schools should aspire to "catch them before they fall" by providing universal screening to students in kindergarten through second grade (12). As the wise reading researcher, Joe Torgesen, once said, "The best solution to the problem of reading failure is to allocate resources for early identification and prevention" (13).

How prevalent is dyslexia screening?

According to the National Center on Improving Literacy, forty-three states have legislation and policies that focus on school-based "universal screening" (14). The ideas inherent in these laws and policies include:

- Screeners aim to locate "at-risk" students as early as possible so potential reading problems can be "headed off" by effective instruction.
- Screening can and should take place in kindergarten and first grade, and possibly other grades.
- Teachers need to know their students' achievement levels on:
  - the most advanced elements of phonological awareness, including phonemic segmentation, blending, and deletion,
  - sound–letter relationships,
  - letter identification,
  - ability to rapidly and automatically name things, from objects and symbols (such as letters) to numbers and colors.
- When students are below achievement benchmarks in screened areas, teachers should teach the deficit skills directly, explicitly, systematically, and repeatedly, using teaching practices (techniques, materials, activities) that are effective for students who struggle to learn to read.
- A student's reading difficulty in the specific areas assessed by screeners might be due to dyslexia.

What elements of literacy do dyslexia screeners assess?

Just as doctors conduct health screenings to check a person for warning signs of a health difficulty, teachers give reading screenings to check students for signs of a reading difficulty. Tests of memory, rapid naming, and phonological awareness are typically included in kindergarten and beginning first-grade screeners. Why? Especially for the last two, deficits in these areas are strong predictors of dyslexia. Also, a school's youngest students are still developing word reading, decoding, and spelling skills. Thus, assessing measures of language outside of these skills is especially informative (15).

Other important testing areas include letter naming fluency (a part of rapid automatic naming), sound–letter associations, oral vocabulary, and word recognition fluency (16). Some screeners, such as the Oklahoma's Dyslexia Checklist for Teachers, are more inclusive than most and consider spelling, comprehension, handwriting, and even directionality and organization (17). Others assess only one domain (such as rapid automatic naming) and should be used in combination with other tests. Additionally, some screeners are pricey (over $400) while others are free!

Regardless of a screener's content and price, it should be 1) easy to give, 2) brief (perhaps taking ten to twenty minutes), 3) developmentally appropriate, and 4) highly predictive of a later reading outcome, meaning the screener is able to identify students who are at risk for not meeting grade-level literacy goals.

Assessment guru David Kilpatrick says phonemic manipulation tasks, especially those involving deleting sounds and substituting sounds, are more sensitive to reading development than other phonological awareness tasks (18). So, to deeply know a student's phonological ability (one of the two best predictors of dyslexia), use phonemic awareness assessments that include phoneme deletion and substitution items. You'll find both types of tasks on Kilpatrick's The PAST Test (see the next section).

What types of screeners are commonly used to check for dyslexia?

There are many screeners, from comprehensive ones designed with dyslexia in mind to others that test only one skill, such as rapid automatic naming or phoneme segmentation and deletion. Some school districts use only one assessment; others use a combination. Here are a few examples of screeners—the list is in no way definitive or supportive of any test.

- *School Age Dyslexia Screener*: Found on the IDA's website, this free screener is the reading subscale of the Colorado Learning Disabilities Questionnaire. It's a six-item questionnaire that teachers complete, with each item rated via a five-point Likert scale (19). Surprisingly, it does not directly address either of the two best predictors of dyslexia—a deficit in phonological awareness skills and a deficit in rapid automatic naming (a proxy for reading fluency).
- *Dynamic Indicators of Basic Early Literacy Skills (DIBELS)*: Developed by the University of Oregon, around since the 1990s, and now in its eighth edition, DIBELS is still used by many districts. After all, it's well studied, exists in both benchmark and

progress monitoring forms, and is free. The assessment includes phonemic segmentation, letter naming fluency, and oral reading fluency, among others (20). It does not delve into phonemic manipulation or the rapid automatic naming of objects, colors, or numbers.

- *The Shaywitz Dyslexia Screen*: Developed by Dr. Sally Shaywitz and published by Pearson, this screener exists as rating forms that emphasize phonological, linguistic, and academic performance (21). It is not free. For K-3 students, the form is completed by teachers. Adolescents complete a self-reported form designed for their population.
- *The Phonemic Awareness Screening Test (PAST):* Developed by David Kilpatrick and updated in 2024, the test of phonological ability is widely used because it's appropriate for many ages (pre-K to adults), it measures phonemic deletion and manipulation, and it's free! The download is quick, the test easy to understand and give. It comes in four forms, which allows you to assess every few months and check for progress (22).
- *Arkansas Rapid Automatized Naming Screener*: Created as a resource for Arkansas Public School teachers, the Arkansas Rapid Automatized Naming Screener (AR-RAN) is an informal universal screener that assesses RAN via color blocks. It comes in two forms, is designed for grades K through two, and, according to the website, "… is a recommended assessment to supplement the Dynamic Indicators of Basic Early Literacy Skills" (23).
- *Acadience Rapid Automatic Naming*: This measure is available as a free download, or it can be purchased from Voyager Sopris Learning. The different forms of the test can be given in kindergarten and first grade, are available in Spanish, and test the rapid automatic naming of objects, letters, and numbers (24).
- *Feifer Assessment of Reading Screening*: Designed to identify students who may be at risk for developmental dyslexia, this screener is based on the original Feifer Assessment of Reading (FAR). It can be given in person or remotely and tests phonemic awareness, rapid automatic naming, and semantic concepts (25). It is not free.

The IDA website also contains a self-administered dyslexia screener for adults. Anyone can take the twenty-three-item questionnaire, each item has a five-point Likert scale, and the scoring guide sits at the bottom. Males have different cut-off scores than females, which is interesting, especially in light of our previous look at brain development differences between young boys and girls and the higher incidence rates of dyslexia (learning disorder) in males (26).

Who formally diagnoses dyslexia?

First, a word of caution. The term *diagnosis* is often associated with medical conditions, as in "I have been diagnosed with cancer and a leaky heart valve." It's true that dyslexia is listed as a learning disorder in the Diagnostic and Statistical Manual-5 (DSM-5), the 1,100-page tome created by the American Psychiatric Association (APA), and this may cause some to think dyslexia is a medical condition that only a medical doctor (such as a pediatrician, neurologist, or psychiatrist) can identify. But dyslexia is not a medical condition nor a state of ill health, and to diagnose it you don't have to have a medical degree. Rather: 1) dyslexia is neurodiversity, 2) one of its major manifestations is it makes learning to read difficult, and 3) it can be identified by a school psychologist or other non-medical evaluator (just as a specific learning disability can be).

Historically, dyslexia evaluations were done outside of school systems. If parents and teachers were concerned that a child might have dyslexia, the onus was on the parents, not the school, to find a professional and pay for an evaluation. Assessors who identified dyslexia (and still do) include educational psychologists, child neurologists, and, especially in very young children, speech pathologists (27, 28). For parents, finding a nearby assessor could be somewhat difficult and the cost of an assessment could run into hundreds, if not thousands, of dollars.

Fortunately, some school districts are beginning to take responsibility for assessing and identifying dyslexia (29, 30). For a school-based evaluation, a school psychologist and/or speech language pathologist administers a battery of assessments (31), just like an evaluator outside of a school district would do. Basing dyslexia evaluations inside a school makes sense for several reasons. First, the evaluation has everything to do with learning to read and nothing to do with medicine. Second, the people who teach reading, and the situations that involve learning written language, are typically found in schools. Finally, school-based dyslexia evaluations are helpful to parents, who interact with nearby schools and pay taxes to fund educational endeavors. There's every reason to think one endeavor could be dyslexia evaluations.

Still, humans and their systems are slow to change. Many districts and their school psychologists continue to identify only specific learning disabilities (SLDs) and speech-language impairments (SLIs), not dyslexia, and the term dyslexia is often absent from a student's Individualized Education Program (IEP). Thus, the children of parents who don't have the resources to proceed with an evaluation through an outside agency might never benefit from information generated by a formal dyslexia evaluation. This situation is unhelpful. Although students with an IEP and a designation of SLD gain the right to the specially designed instruction that can help them overcome their reading difficulties, these students are often still in the dark about *why* they are having great difficulties learning to read and spell.

Q A Can a student be both gifted and dyslexic?

Yes. Gifted students can also have dyslexia.

Sometimes called twice exceptional, these children are often curious and creative, have strong reasoning and critical thinking abilities, and possess a good deal of vocabulary and background knowledge. Interestingly, when teachers and parents focus too much on these students' strengths, they often miss the depths of their reading deficits (32).

In my book, *How to Prevent Reading Difficulties, Grades PreK-3: Proactive Practices for Teaching Young Children to Read* (33), I present a case study of a fourth-grade student who was being considered for the gifted program, even as his reading achievement scores were in the second percentile. This nine-year-old boy loved math, could talk extensively about the workings of a black hole, understood the ins and outs of the Harry Potter books (when he listened to them being read out loud), and had a difficult time fluently reading *The Cat in the Hat*. From kindergarten through third grade, his school system had provided "help" and "interventions," given him As and Bs in reading on his report card, and allowed him to pass from one grade to the next. But in fourth grade, he began to completely fail his reading-based subjects and became very frustrated. His mother, a medical doctor, took him to an outside evaluator, who identified dyslexia. She then enrolled him in an intensive after-school tutoring program. By the beginning of his seventh-grade year, he was reading on grade level.

Why is a formal evaluation important?

As touched on earlier, an evaluation identifies the origins of a reading difficulty. This allows a teacher and a school system to provide, connect, and fine tune the Tier I, II, and III instruction that ultimately helps the student overcome their difficulties. Also, an effective evaluation documents the history of the student's reading difficulties. This can then play an important role when it comes to determining a student's eligibility for services, including special education. Finally, and perhaps most importantly, an evaluation helps teachers, parents, and students understand the nature of a reading difficulty.

I've personally met teachers who are also parents of children with dyslexia, and they've told me an identification was tremendously important to them, their child, and the school system. An evaluation helps parents understand the reality of their child's situation and plan for their future. It gives teachers a clear understanding of the student's strengths and weaknesses and helps them instruct in ways that lead to the student's success and happiness. And it helps a child truly understand themselves: why they struggle in certain situations, what their strengths and weaknesses are, who they are as a person, and how they want to be in the world.

How much does a formal evaluation cost and how long might it take?

When a school psychologist evaluates a student and determines that they have a specific learning disability, the evaluation is taxpayer funded. So, in a sense, it's free of charge. Obviously, the same is true if a school psychologist conducts a dyslexia evaluation and renders an identification.

As for formal evaluations outside of a school system, information on their cost and time varies wildly depending on the source. The Yale Center for Dyslexia & Creativity is vague about the cost and perhaps excessive regarding the time, saying: "Evaluations can be expensive" and "Evaluations often take place over two days, with about four to five hours of testing each day" (34).

Some centers associated with the organization Scottish Rite for Children, such as the Luke Waites Center for Dyslexia and Learning Disorders in Dallas, offer a complete dyslexia evaluation that is free of charge and done in "… two to four hours depending on [the] child's age and academic needs" (35). Places like the Luke Waites Center, however, are few and far between and families must apply for an evaluation slot.

A 2022 Reddit dyslexia discussion thread showed people quoting evaluation prices and times that ranged from $5,000 for a "full two-day neuropsychological evaluation" to a $995 telehealth evaluation with a licensed clinical psychologist that "took a total of 4 hours over two sessions" (36). And personally speaking, I've had parents tell me their child's evaluation cost $800, $1,500, and $2,000, and that it took a lot of effort to find an evaluator.

What are the components of a formal evaluation of dyslexia?

It's important to note that no two evaluators or evaluation centers will test for dyslexia in the same way. Nevertheless, an evaluation should always be comprehensive, assessing intellectual ability, academic achievement, and the underlying language skills that are closely linked to dyslexia. In addition, all other causes of reading difficulties should be ruled out, from missing school and multi-language learning to autism or an intellectual disability.

These two tables show possible areas for testing and information gathering (37, 38, 39). The first table is specific to literacy, the second lists non-literacy factors associated with dyslexia.

TABLE 3.1

<table>
<tr><th>General Literacy Area</th><th colspan="5">Specific Skills</th></tr>
<tr><td rowspan="2">Oral Language</td><td>Phoneme segmenting and blending</td><td>Sound ID (first and last)</td><td>Sound deletion (syllable to phoneme)</td><td>Identifying and generating rhyming words</td><td>Rapid automatic naming (of colors, objects, letters)</td></tr>
<tr><td colspan="5">• Understand an age-appropriate story and spoken directions.
• Understand and use words that are age appropriate.</td></tr>
<tr><td>Reading</td><td>Ability to read nonsense words</td><td>Ability to read common "sight words," such as they, him, because, again</td><td colspan="2">Fluency on word lists
Fluency with sentence reading (accuracy, rate, prosody)</td><td>Comprehension
Ability to comprehend a short passage
Comprehension information regarding longer texts, like books</td></tr>
</table>

(Continued)

General Literacy Area	*Specific Skills*
Spelling	• Spelling of simple "sight words," like *be*, *the*, *and*, *was*. • Spelling words using sounds and patterns, from CVC (*cat*, *mop*) and CCVC (*slap*, *grit*) to more complex syllable types (vowel digraphs, consonant diagraphs), up to and including multisyllable words. • Spelling nonsense words.
Writing	• Cold writing sample. For example, "Write two sentences that tell me something about yourself." • Combining sentences to show grammatical and syntactical knowledge. For example, "Combine these two sentences into one sentence – The dog is big. The dog barks."
Background knowledge	• General world knowledge. • Vocabulary knowledge, tested both orally and through reading.

TABLE 3.2

General Area	*Specific Area or Note About the Test*
Intelligence	• Some may give a general test of intelligence, as measured by a Woodcock-Johnson or WISC-R. • Some may gauge this via school reports (past achievement in school, current achievement in school or job situation).
Family history	• Reports of reading/spelling difficulties across generations in the family.
Young child history	• Prenatal and birth history. • Delays/difficulties acquiring speech/language.
School history	• Changes in schools (relocating frequently, multiple teacher changes, etc.). • Attendance data. • History of tutoring or interventions. • Response to tutoring and interventions.

If a profile emerges that is characteristic of readers with dyslexia, then a diagnosis of dyslexia will be given. From there, an IEP or 504 plan will be developed. More on this follows in the next chapter.

What formal assessments might an evaluator give?

Every skill area listed previously has more than one test that can evaluate it. While clinicians trained in different ways use different assessments, still, some tests rise to the top of everyone's list. For example, the University of Michigan's Dyslexia Help website gives fourteen dyslexia assessments clinicians tend to like (40). If you're a reading nerd like me, you might be interested in these assessments and perhaps enjoy reading through their sometimes-amusing acronyms, like TAPS and GORT-5 (my favorite).

The University of Michigan: Fourteen Dyslexia Assessments

Here are just a few of the most common assessments from their collection. You can find the entire list at the QR code provided.

Test	*What It Tests*
CTOPP-2 Comprehensive Test of Phonological Processing	Phonological awareness, phonemic segmentation and blending, phonemic deletion, rapid automatic naming (symbols and non-symbols).
GORT-5 Gray Oral Reading Test	Oral reading rate, accuracy, and fluency. Also, comprehension and an oral reading index, which is a composite of fluency and comprehension.
TAPS Test of Auditory Processing Skills	Phonological processing, auditory memory, and listening comprehension.
TWS-5 Test of Written Spelling	A dictated-word format in two forms. Takes about twenty minutes to give, individually or in groups. Each form has fifty spelling words collected from a variety of basal spelling series and graded word lists.

Is an identification of dyslexia helpful?

Typically, yes.

Labels, which flow from diagnoses or identifications, do have their downsides. One might be that a label reduces the whole of a student to two or three words. For example, when a child is described as a "learning disabled student," the label tends to take over, eclipsing through omission the abilities that are part of every child. This is one reason person-first nomenclature is preferred—a student with autism vs. an autistic student, a student with dyslexia as opposed to a dyslexic student. Another downside might be this: when poorly understood, labels can lead to social stigmas—negative ideas or attitudes about others that can lead to disapproval, separation, bullying, and discrimination.

More often, though, my sense is that identification and a label leads to positive outcomes. Knowing that a child is "a student with dyslexia" can lead to heightened awareness—for teachers, parents, society, and especially those who have the condition. Through heightened awareness comes a sense of understanding and agency—"I know what this is, and I know what I can do about it."

It's true that effective reading instruction, from general classroom teaching to Tier III interventions, can and should occur whether a struggling student has dyslexia or not. Instruction is not label dependent. But a formal diagnosis or identification of dyslexia helps everyone understand and accept that there is a learning problem specific to reading and that the problem is not due to laziness, ineffective parenting, or misguided teaching. Putting a name on the difficulty—dyslexia—also helps everyone realize that although this difficulty will always be with the person, so will the person's strengths.

Dyslexia researcher, Dr. Guinevere Eden, puts it this way:

> ... I think it's really important for these kids to understand what their dyslexia is and what it means for them... it's important for people with dyslexia to let people know what it is so that they understand what it is they need as learners (41).

***

Because determining dyslexia is a complex endeavor, many people will be called upon to play a role in the evaluation process, including classroom teachers. In this chapter we looked at how teachers can help to screen students for dyslexia, what those screeners could be, and what literacy areas are most sensitive to predicting dyslexia. We also learned that teachers will most likely be asked to collect evaluation information from a variety of sources, including behavior checklists, screening scores, and numerous literacy-related assessments, like spelling tests, writing samples, and oral reading fluency probes. Finally, we examined who might give formal assessments capable of diagnosing or identifying dyslexia.

In the next chapter, we'll look at who is responsible for teaching a student with dyslexia, what are a student's options for instruction outside of the general education classroom, and why an "everyone helps" approach is much more effective than a "gate keeping" approach.

End of Chapter Resources

1 International Dyslexia Association. 2008. "Testing and Evaluation." International Dyslexia Association. https://dyslexiaida.org/testing-and-evaluation/.

2 International Dyslexia Association. 2008. "Testing and Evaluation." International Dyslexia Association. https://dyslexiaida.org/testing-and-evaluation/.

3 Consortium on Reaching Excellence in Education. 2018. "Understanding Dyslexia: Why Early Prevention and Intervention are Crucial." www.corelearn.com/wp-content/uploads/2018/01/understanding-dyslexia-whitepaper.pdf.

4 Gaab, Nadine. 2017. "It's a Myth That Young Children Cannot Be Screened for Dyslexia." International Dyslexia Association. http://dyslexiaida.org/its-a-myth-that-young-children-cannot-be-screened-for-dyslexia/.

5 Gaab, Nadine. 2017. "It's a Myth That Young Children Cannot Be Screened for Dyslexia." International Dyslexia Association. http://dyslexiaida.org/its-a-myth-that-young-children-cannot-be-screened-for-dyslexia/.

6 Puolakanaho, Anne, et al. 2007. "Very Early Phonological and Language Skills: Estimating Individual Risk of Reading Disability." *Journal of Child Psychology and Psychiatry* 48 (9): 923–931.

7 Kraft, Indra, et al. 2016. "Predicting Early Signs of Dyslexia at a Preliterate Age By Combining Behavioral Assessment With Structural MRI." *Neuroimage* 143: 378–386.

8 Torgesen, Joseph. 2004. "Avoiding the Devastating Downward Spiral: The Evidence That Early Intervention Prevents Reading Failure." *American Educator*. www.aft.org/ae/fall2004/torgesen.

9 International Dyslexia Association. "Universal Screening: K-2 Reading Fact Sheet." International Dyslexia Association. https://dyslexiaida.org/universal-screening-k-2-reading/.

10 On the Brain: The Harvard Mahony Neuroscience Institute Letter. 2014. "Tackling Dyslexia at an Early Age" 20 (3): 1–2. https://hms.harvard.edu/sites/default/files/publications%20archive/

OnTheBrain/OnTheBrainFall14.pdf?fbclid=IwAR3FdX8UNRs7qh6KI_0K03zzFKaSGoc9sLbR5PM5EdBqUCI6ZGWckEkOV6U.
11 Lyon, Reid, and Jack Fletcher. 2006. "Early Warning System." Education Matters. www.educationnext.org/early-warning-system/.
12 Torgesen, Joseph. 1998. "Catch Them Before They Fall: Identification and Assessment to Prevent Reading Failure in Young Children." *American Educator*. Spring–Summer, 1–8. www.aft.org/sites/default/files/torgesen.pdf.
13 Torgesen, Joseph. 2004. "Lessons Learned from Research on Interventions for Students Who Have Difficulty Learning to Read." In *The Voice of Evidence in Reading Research*, ed. P. McCardle and V. Chhabra. Baltimore, MD: Paul H. Brookes Publishing Co., p. 355.
14 National Center on Improving Literacy. 2024. "State of Dyslexia: Screening Policies." National Center on Improving Literacy. https://improvingliteracy.org/state-of-dyslexia/.
15 Compton, Donald, et al. 2010. "Selecting At-Risk First Grade Readers For Early Intervention: Eliminating False Positives and Exploring the Promise of a Two-Stage Gated Screening Process." *Journal of Educational Psychology* 102 (2): 327–340.
16 Jenkins, Joseph, and Evelyn Johnson. 2024. "Universal Screening for Reading Problems: Why and How Should We Do This?" RTI Action Network. https://decodingdyslexiaca.org/wp-content/uploads/2018/01/RTI-Action-Network_Why_and_How.pdf.
17 Oklahoma Department of Education. 2024. "Dyslexia Checklist for Teachers." Oklahoma Dyslexia and Dysgraphia Handbook Appendix. https://oklahoma.gov/content/dam/ok/en/osde/documents/services/special-education/dyslexia/OK%20Dyslexia%20and%20Dysgraphia%20Handbook_V2.pdf.
18 Kilpatrick, David. 2015. *The Essentials of Assessing, Preventing, and Overcoming Reading Difficulties*. Hoboken, NJ: Wiley & Sons, p. 179.
19 International Dyslexia Association. 2024. "School Age Dyslexia Screener." International Dyslexia Association. https://dyslexiaida.org/screening-for-dyslexia/dyslexia-screener-for-school-age-children/.
20 University of Oregon. 2024. "DIBELS (8th edition)." University of Oregon. https://dibels.uoregon.edu/materials/dibels.
21 Shaywitz, Sally E. 2021. "Shaywitz DyslexiaScreen." Pearson. www.pearsonassessments.com/store/usassessments/en/Store/Professional-Assessments/MTSS-RTI-PBIS-Benchmarking/Shaywitz-DyslexiaScreen/p/100001918.html#:~:text=The%20Shaywitz%20

DyslexiaScreen%20emphasizes%20phonological,of%20past%20and%20current%20performance.

22 The PAST Test. 2024. "Phonemic Awareness Screening Test." The PAST Test. https://thepasttest.com

23 Arkansas Department of Education. 2024. "Arkansas Rapid Automatic Naming Screener." Arkansas Department of Education. https://dese.ade.arkansas.gov/Files/20201221160134_Arkansas_Rapid_Naming_Screener.pdf.

24 Acadience Learning. 2024. "Acadience RAN." Acadience Learning. https://acadiencelearning.org/acadience-reading/acadience-ran/?highlight=Rapid%20automatic%20naming.

25 PAR. 2024. "Feifer Assessment of Reading Screening." PAR. www.parinc.com/products/FAR-SCREEN.

26 International Dyslexia Association. 2024. "Dyslexia Screener for Adults." International Dyslexia Association. https://dyslexiaida.org/screening-for-dyslexia/dyslexia-screener-for-adults/.

27 The Yale Center for Dyslexia & Creativity. 2024. "Dyslexia Evaluation Overview." The Yale Center for Dyslexia & Creativity. https://dyslexia.yale.edu/resources/parents/what-parents-can-do/dyslexia-evaluation-overview/.

28 Decoding Dyslexia Pennsylvania. 2024. "Understanding IEP Evaluations." Decoding Dyslexia Pennsylvania. https://decodingdyslexiapa.com/advocate/understanding-iep-evaluations/.

29 Decoding Dyslexia Pennsylvania. 2024. "Understanding IEP Evaluations." Decoding Dyslexia Pennsylvania. https://decodingdyslexiapa.com/advocate/understanding-iep-evaluations/.

30 International Dyslexia Association. 2024. "Testing and Evaluation." International Dyslexia Association. https://dyslexiaida.org/testing-and-evaluation/.

31 Viscomi, Cori. 2018. "The Speech-Language Pathologists Role in Diagnosing Dyslexia." ASHA Wire. https://leader.pubs.asha.org/do/10.1044/the-speech-language-pathologists-role-in-diagnosing-dyslexia/full/.

32 National Association for Gifted Children. 2009. "Twice Exceptionality White Paper." National Association for Gifted Children. www.nagc.org/news/the-role-of-assessments-in-the-identification-of-gifted-students .

33 Weakland, Mark. 2021. *How to Prevent Reading Difficulties, Grades PreK-3: Proactive Practices for Teaching Young Children to Read.* Thousand Oaks, CA: Corwin Press.

34 The Yale Center for Dyslexia & Creativity. 2024. "Dyslexia Evaluation Overview." The Yale Center for Dyslexia & Creativity. https://dyslexia.yale.edu/resources/parents/what-parents-can-do/dyslexia-evaluation-overview/.
35 Scottish Rite for Children. 2024. "Dyslexia: The Evaluation Process." Scottish Rite for Children. https://scottishriteforchildren.org/dyslexia-the-evaluation-process/.
36 Reddit. 2024. "How Much Did You Pay for Your Assessment?" Reddit. www.reddit.com/r/Dyslexia/comments/11jnqdy/how_much_did_you_pay_for_your_assessment/?rdt=39643.
37 Understood. 2017. "Inside a Dyslexia Evaluation." YouTube video, 20:43. www.youtube.com/watch?v=DNu4WiQaVTI.
38 International Dyslexia Association. 2024. "Testing and Evaluation." International Dyslexia Association. https://dyslexiaida.org/testing-and-evaluation/.
39 The Yale Center for Dyslexia & Creativity. 2024. "Dyslexia Evaluation Overview." The Yale Center for Dyslexia & Creativity. https://dyslexia.yale.edu/resources/parents/what-parents-can-do/dyslexia-evaluation-overview/.
40 Dyslexia Help. 2024. "Fourteen Tests Dyslexia Clinicians Like." University of Michigan https://dyslexiahelp.umich.edu/professionals/learn-about-dyslexia/diagnosing-dyslexia/tests/14-dyslexia-tests-clinicians-like#:~:text=We%20find%20the%20CTOPP%2D2,skills%20and%2C%20thus%2C%20dyslexi.
41 Reading Rockets. 2024. "Profile: Guinevere Eden." Reading Rockets. www.readingrockets.org/people-and-organizations/guinevere-eden.

CHAPTER 4

Everyone Can Help Students with Dyslexia

Knowing difficult situations abound, Fred Rogers, a.k.a. Mr. Rogers, had words of wisdom for kids. "Look for the helpers," he'd say. "You will always find people who are helping." Fortunately for students, schools are full of helpers, from teachers and custodians to administrators and parent volunteers. Equally true is this: everyone in a school can help students with dyslexia, especially classroom teachers.

A teacher's kind words and welcoming smile are surely a huge help to every child who encounters them. In this chapter, however, we'll delve into something more specific, namely literacy instruction. Our topics include the roles of grade-level teachers, special education teachers and reading interventionists; what gatekeeping is and how it can be overcome; and 504 plans and Individualized Education Program (IEP) meetings. Along the way, we'll celebrate the ways teachers, through their helping, diminish the difficulties of others, for when they employ instructional practices that benefit students with dyslexia, classroom teachers also more effectively teach all their students the reading, writing, and spelling skills they need.

Can I help a student with dyslexia learn to read within my general education classroom?

Yes. To what degree depends upon the intensity of the dyslexia and the support systems available to both teacher and student.

A child with mild dyslexia can certainly learn to read within a well-taught general education classroom. The key phrase is "well-taught," meaning that the teacher employs all manner of effective practices, from formative assessment and progress monitoring to high expectations, differentiation, and a variety of activities, materials, and instructional techniques that thoroughly teach foundational literacy skills. The next chapter will describe some of these practices.

For students with moderate to severe dyslexia, their challenges may be so great that they'll need additional instruction in a small group setting with a special educator, reading interventionist, or dyslexia specialist, and this instruction will most likely be given outside of the regular education classroom. But remember, this specialized teaching should *supplement* rather than supplant general classroom instruction.

When addressing all manner of reading difficulties, including those caused by dyslexia, it is helpful to have a robust and well-connected support system in place, one that includes knowledgeable and effective general education teachers, reading specialists, and interventionists outside the general classroom, and parents and community organizations that support children with things like homework, tutoring, and specialized reading programs.

Will a student diagnosed with dyslexia *always* be placed in a special education program or in a reading intervention group?

No.

When predictors of dyslexia are identified at a young age *and* effective reading practices are employed, reading difficulties can be overcome and even prevented. This means that some students might never need to leave a general education classroom to see a reading interventionist or special education teacher.

To receive special education services via an IEP, a student must first have an identified disability, such as dyslexia or specific learning disability (SLD). But even with a diagnosed SLD, a student might not qualify for special education services. Why? Simply put, if a student is making appropriate educational gains in a regular education setting, they don't need special education (1).

It's interesting to note that some students with moderate to severe reading difficulties can learn mostly or even exclusively within a general education classroom. I lived this reality for three years when I ran a co-taught Tier I reading program for third graders who were significantly below reading benchmarks. Each year, a few of the kids had an IEP but most did not. Only a quarter to a third received a Tier III intervention that was beyond their general education program. True, our classroom was different in that it was co-taught by a reading interventionist (me) and a grade-level educator (my co-op teacher). But the highly effective reading instruction we gave was what any typical third-grade student could and should receive, meaning the children received direct and explicit instruction, integrated and systematic spelling and phonics taught to mastery, a mixture of whole group and small group teaching, and lots of independent practice in reading and writing. My co-teacher and I taught in a way that moved more than 90 percent of our historically low-achieving students to at *least* a year's worth of growth in reading, writing, and spelling, as measured by various benchmark assessments. If administration had also implemented this effective teaching model in first and second grade, our school would most likely have prevented many serious reading difficulties from ever occurring.

Q A If I suspect one of my students has dyslexia, should I hold off on targeted instruction until a diagnosis is given?

Emphatically, no!

If you are a teacher who knows what dyslexia is and can recognize its signs in a student in your classroom, then you are the perfect person to take instructional action right now. The big idea is this: don't ever wait to provide interventions! And don't ever think that reading interventions are the responsibility of only reading interventionists and special education teachers.

If your student is already receiving Tier II or III interventions outside of your classroom, talk to the interventionist (reading teacher, special education teacher, speech-language pathologist) and find ways to integrate some of their content and instruction into your whole group and small group teaching. Here are four examples: 1) start each spelling-phonics lesson with ten minutes of direct and explicit instruction on one or two specific spelling-phonic patterns; 2) fold in multi-sensory teaching techniques; 3) add highly decodable books to your small group instruction and classroom library, and 4) differentiate your weekly list of spelling words, providing lots of pattern practice for the student you suspect has dyslexia. None of these actions will hurt your highfliers and all of them will help any student who struggles to read, including the student who may have dyslexia.

If your student does not receive help outside of your classroom, then analyze your formative assessment data, decide on what foundational skills your student needs, and teach these skills to the student, especially during small group instruction. For example, if your student needs to build automatic word recognition, provide more reading repetitions during your whole group instruction by regularly picking a story passage and re-reading it using I Read, We Read, You Read. Then during your small group instruction, provide more spelling-phonic practice and decodable text, and again, keep your instruction direct and explicit. Give your student one extra small group session per week. And monitor the student's progress with reading probes every three weeks. If appropriate progress isn't happening, discuss next steps with your student support team. These steps would most likely include continuing what you are doing, adding an upper tier intervention, and starting a dyslexia evaluation process.

I'm a general education teacher who has a student with dyslexia in my classroom. I have no training in how to teach this student. What do I do?

First, keep reading this book! You've already gained useful knowledge in the first four chapters and Chapters 5 and 6 are full of practical yet effective teaching techniques, phonic activities, spelling strategies, classroom accommodations, and more. Second, meet with your school's special education teacher or reading interventionist and "pick their brains." Even better, work to have them come into your room, if even for a short amount of time, and teach some model lessons. Conversely, arrange to go and sit in on a few of their lessons. Then do some of the things they do in your classroom.

Here's something else: as you teach *all* your students, you may already be employing practices that are effective for children who have dyslexia. These practices include direct and explicit instruction, multi-sensory teaching, whole group instruction with differentiation, small group instruction, teaching only one unknown at a time, and repeatedly practicing skills to ensure mastery. An additional thing you can do is increase the frequency and duration of these practices.

It's especially important to consider frequency and duration because students who have moderate to severe dyslexia may need dozens, if not hundreds, of repetitions to master phoneme discrimination, sound–letter associations, and the automatic recognition of words. So, you'll have to find many ways to repeatedly present the same content. Differentiation, multi-sensory learning, small group instruction, and multiple activities that teach the same skill or concept are essential.

If you aren't doing these practices, please do them. If you don't know how or have forgotten how to do specific instructional techniques and activities, one place to begin (and it is only a start) is my YouTube Channel, Mark Weakland Literacy. There you can watch one-, two-, and three-minute videos that demonstrate phonological, spelling, and phonic activities that are done in a direct and explicit instructional style and often involve a multi-sensory element. Even better, get with a highly qualified teacher who does these practices, learn from them, and do what they do.

Once identified, is a student with dyslexia the responsibility of the special education teacher or the reading interventionist?

Neither.

First a word—*gatekeeping*—and a definition. Gatekeeping is when a student with a disability, such as autism, attention deficit disorder (ADD), or dyslexia, is limited in their ability to access and participate in general classroom environments or participate in broader activities within a school (2). Some define gatekeeping more broadly, including factors like systemic racism or gender bias, which inhibit or even prohibit entire groups from participating in certain pursuits.

Gatekeeping exists on a continuum from subtle to blatant. It occurs when a child with cerebral palsy or Down's syndrome is discouraged from attending a particular school ("we don't provide services for those children here") and when older students attending schools with high rates of free and reduced lunch have little to no access to Advanced Placement (AP) courses. It also happens when teachers expect any student with a specific learning disability (dyslexia) to *always* see a reading interventionist or special education teacher for the bulk, or even all, of their literacy instruction.

While there is no doubt that some students will benefit from additional, targeted instruction with a specialist (such as a special education teacher or reading interventionist), there is also no doubt that the same children will benefit when general classroom instruction connects to and reinforces the instruction from the specialist. Therefore, a student with dyslexia is the responsibility of *all* teachers, including the general education teacher.

Additionally, it is the responsibility of administrators to help make every teacher's instruction as successful as possible. Effective instruction should never be found only in Tier II and III settings. Among other effects, strong teaching *everywhere* helps minimize the chance that gatekeeping will occur *anywhere*. So, for a variety of reasons, school systems should aspire to support all teachers, from interventionists to classroom instructors, and *connect* the tiers so that everyone is using instructional practices (such as repetition, error correction, the direct and explicit instruction of learning strategies) that benefit all learners, especially the ones that struggle the most.

What is an IEP and why might a student with dyslexia have one?

An Individualized Education Plan (IEP) is just what it sounds like: an education plan tailored to one student's unique needs. An IEP is for any student who has a disability recognized under the Individuals with Disabilities Education Act (IDEA). Disability categories under IDEA include but are not limited to the following: autism, deafness, emotional disturbance, intellectual disability, and specific learning disability, which encompasses dyslexia (3).

According to the revised Individuals with Disabilities Education Act of 2024, an IEP should "… be a statement of the child's present levels of academic achievement and functional performance," give "… measurable annual goals, including academic and functional goals designed to meet the child's needs," and "… enable the child to be involved in and make progress in the general education curriculum" (4). An IEP is like a map for educators. The destinations are yearly goals that are based on a student's abilities and achieved via the specialized instruction spelled out in the IEP. The instruction is often, but not exclusively, given by a special education teacher. The IEP also lists classroom accommodations that help students achieve their goals and feel more comfortable in a regular education setting.

To receive an IEP, a student with dyslexia (who has a specific learning disability) must need specialized designed instruction to make progress in the general education curriculum. This specialized instruction will then be carried out by a special education teacher, a reading interventionist, a general education teacher, or some combination thereof.

What is a 504 plan?

The roots of 504 plans are in the Rehabilitation Act of 1973, the United States' first major federal disability rights law (5). Section 504 of this act forbids organizations (like schools) and employers from excluding or denying individuals with disabilities an equal opportunity to receive program benefits and services (6). Applied to a public education setting, Section 504 means a child with a legal diagnosis (such as dyslexia) who is attending either an elementary or secondary school is entitled to accommodations that will ensure their academic success.

A 504 plan is specifically for general education students who do *not* qualify for special education services and thus will not have an IEP that lists specially designed instruction and classroom accommodations. Here are examples of some 504 plan accommodations that a teacher could provide to a student with dyslexia.

Delivery of information (teaching) accommodations	• Allow keyboarding for tasks typically done in handwriting. • Provide text-to-speech and/or speech-to-text technology. • Give ample time to complete reading assignments. • Provide tape-recorded lectures. • Don't require students to copy information from the board. • Allow information to be accessed or reported on using a different format (for example, listening to an audio book rather than reading written text).
Assessment accommodations	• Give tests in small group settings. • Allow for answer choices to be given orally. • Give breaks during assessment. • Reduce the number of words on a spelling test. • Reduce the number of word problems on a math test. • Refrain from grading writing assignments based on spelling errors.

What does a teacher do at a 504 plan or IEP meeting?

One thing teachers do is go to meetings: faculty meetings, parent–teacher meetings, student support meetings, meetings to review your classroom performance and debate your union contract. Sure as the sun shines, at some point you'll be asked to attend a 504 plan or IEP meeting for a student with dyslexia. Besides yourself, the following people may be in attendance: parents, administrators, other teachers, a child advocate, behavioral support staff, a school psychologist, a speech-language therapist.

Classroom teachers have a special and important role to play in the development and implementation of an IEP or 504 plan. One reason is that a classroom teacher probably spends more time than anyone (except a parent) with a child who has dyslexia. This means they know more than just reading scores; they know the student's personality, interests, quirks, thinking styles, and strengths and needs in multiple subject areas.

As a classroom teacher, your offerings at an IEP or 504 plan meeting might include any or all of the following:

- Anecdotal information on the student's personality and classroom behaviors.
- Scores that show present level of academic performance in multiple subject areas and observations on how the student performs on classwork.
- An opinion about what is obtainable for the student. In other words, you can help the team, especially the special education teacher, formulate achievable IEP or 504 plan goals.
- Suggestions for classroom materials, activities, and routines that can help the student reach the IEP or 504 plan goals.
- Your opinion on what is reasonable and possible in your classroom regarding accommodations, instruction, and curriculum. You can also discuss the supports *you* will need, which might include training, planning time, and materials.

***

Teaching math and science, monitoring hallways, instilling manners, participating in school assemblies, meeting with parents, submitting grades and lesson plans… the list of what teachers do is seemingly endless. So, when you read in this chapter that teachers can also assist in evaluations and teach students with significant reading difficulties, you may have felt burdened, overwhelmed, or both. This seems only natural.

Hopefully, as you reflect on this chapter and move to the next, you will become inspired with a feeling of "I can do this." As we know, teachers literally provide children with lifelines, giving kindness, shelter, and stability, as well as the factual knowledge and actionable skills that, at the very least, give kids a chance at having a safe and comfortable life. This is especially true for the students who have a difficult time learning to read, write, and spell.

Another reason you might come to feel "I can do this" is that you now see how the evaluation process, and the instruction that flows from it, dovetails with what you are already doing in your classroom, as well as what you aspire to do. Effective instruction that works for students who struggle a lot also works for students who struggle just a bit, and it certainly won't hurt the children who learn to read quickly and easily.

In this chapter, we learned that everyone in a school can help students with dyslexia, especially grade-level classroom teachers. Specific ways of helping include giving effective Tier I instruction, coordinating with special education teachers and reading interventionists, and attending 504 plans or IEP meetings. In the next chapter, we'll dive into the details of instruction, looking at activities that connect across the tiers, utilize effective practices, and teach phonology, spelling, phonics, and more.

End of Chapter Resources

1 Lindstrom, Jennifer. 2019. "Dyslexia in the Schools: Assessment and Identification." *Teaching Exceptional Children* 51 (3): 189–200.

2 Cambridge University Press and Assessment. 2025. "Gatekeeping." OnlineDictionary. https://dictionary.cambridge.org/us/dictionary/english/gatekeeping.

3 Congressional Research Service. 2024. "The Individuals with Disabilities Education Act (IDEA), Part B: Key Statutory and Regulatory Provisions." congress.gov. https://crsreports.congress.gov/product/pdf/R/R41833.

4 Congressional Research Service. 2024. "The Individuals with Disabilities Education Act (IDEA), Part B: Key Statutory and Regulatory Provisions." congress.gov. https://crsreports.congress.gov/product/pdf/R/R41833.

5 GovInfo. 2024. "Employment Protections Under the Rehabilitation Act of 1973: 50 Years of Protecting Americans with Disabilities in the Workplace." GovInfo. www.govinfo.gov/app/details/USCODE-2011-title29/USCODE-2011-title29-chap16-subchapV-sec793.

6 Department of Health and Human Services. 2024. "Fact Sheet: Your Rights Under Section 504 of the Rehabilitation Act (H-8/June 2000 – revised June 2006)." Department of Health and Human Services. www.hhs.gov/sites/default/files/ocr/civilrights/resources/factsheets/504.pdf.

CHAPTER 5

We Can Teach Students with Dyslexia to Read, Write, and Spell

Reading is a miraculous combination of sound, sight, and meaning. To become readers, students must hear and understand language, associate the spoken sounds of a language with written symbols (letters), store in their brains the correct letter sequences and meanings of dozens of words, and acquire the ability to automatically retrieve these "brain words" as they encounter them in text. As their development continues, students eventually become fluent. Easily reading sentence after sentence, they experience words not as individual drops, but as a meaningful river, overflowing with connections, emotion, and personal significance. This flow is enabled and enhanced by topical knowledge, life experiences that provide background knowledge, and the use of reading strategies, from self-monitoring to making predictions and summarizing.

Students with dyslexia have an especially difficult time storing and automatically retrieving words. This, in turn, can limit their understanding of text. To help them overcome their challenges, teachers must give instruction that is more direct, targeted, and multi-dimensional than what might typically be given. Still, this instruction shouldn't spring from nothingness.

Rather, it should be a foundational way of teaching, given to *all* students at varying times and in differing amounts. When teaching students with dyslexia, teachers boost, focus, and adjust the effective teaching techniques, classroom materials, and curricular content that is already there.

If you are currently using a program that is ineffective for teaching your lowest-achieving students, this chapter will be especially helpful—you can implement some of the ideas and practices on Monday morning, add more later, and refine everything over time. If your program is already successfully teaching the students who struggle the most, then you're in the "win-win" zone. Simply put this chapter's tools in your toolbox and use them when needed.

No matter their age, from five to fifteen, students who are learning to become fluent readers *must* reach the point where they automatically recognize almost every word they encounter in a text. When you use the specific practices in this chapter, as well as generally embrace structured literacy's way of teaching (more on this in a bit), you will help all your students build foundational skills, especially the ones who have or may have dyslexia.

When teaching phonology, spelling, and phonics to students with dyslexia, what instructional techniques should I use?

Use the same techniques you employ when teaching students who do not have dyslexia! But use them with greater frequency and duration. Highly effective teaching techniques include:

Repeated Practice

For students with dyslexia, spelling and phonics are especially difficult to master. Therefore, you'll need to give more repetitions in these areas (1, 2). To keep your students engaged during the repetitions, vary the activities that present the content (see later sections in this chapter). In effect, you'll repeat the same content many times but present it in multiple ways through differing activities.

As the ancient Latin saying goes, "*Repetitio est mater studiorum,*" meaning "Repetition is the mother of learning." Centuries later, Dr. Samuel Orton and educator Anna Gillingham called the idea of repeated practice "Relentless redundancy."

Distributed Practice

This means break large blocks of practice into small amounts, spread across the weeks, days, and hours (3). For example, instead of giving a thirty-five-minute phonics lesson three times a week, teach phonics daily. Each day, do phonics for fifteen minutes and then do something else like reading connected text. Later, circle back for ten more minutes of phonics. In this way you give more phonics, more regularly, in smaller doses. Also, as the week progresses, review all that was learned and add small bits of new information. Along the way, formatively assess. Is your student mastering the information?

Direct and Explicit Instruction

Don't ask students to guess and don't assume they will naturally learn correct information on their own. Instead, deliberately and explicitly give students all facts, concepts, and skills, and have them interact with the learning continuously. For example, don't visually and orally present the words *coin*, *join*, and *toil* and then ask, "What part of the words do you think says/oi/?" Rather, do something like this: present the digraph OI and say, "Together the letters O and I say/oi/. Say that sound with me/oi/. You say it/oi/. The sound/oi/is spelled OI. How is/oi/spelled? [Students respond.] Look at these three words. The/oi/sound is spelled OI. Point to the letters OI in each word. [Students respond.] Listen and watch as I read each word. [Teacher reads.] You read the words. [Students read.] How is the/oi/sound spelled? [Students respond.]"

For multi-language learners (MLLs) who have dyslexia, strong foundational literacy skills in their native language is what helps them attain literacy skills in English (4). To help achieve this, it is suggested that MLL teachers provide students with direct instruction in sound–symbol connections (5). This is by no means easy. The specific challenges schools face include a lack of teachers who can provide specialized instruction to MLL students in their native tongue, as well as the multitude of languages that are sometimes spoken in classrooms. But in schools with a high concentration of one non-English language (Spanish, for example), a specially designed Orton-Gillingham-esque program might be a possible solution (6).

Instant Error Correction

Like direct and explicit instruction, instant error correction increases the chance that information and skills will be stored perfectly and permanently in the brain (7, 8). The basic idea is that whenever a student makes a mistake, stop them, give the correct response, and have them practice it. So, if a child encounters the sentence "The bellhop pushed the cart" and says, "The boy pushed the cart," don't allow them to keep going. Rather, stop at the mistake point and teach *bellhop*. The teaching can include a reminder to look at every letter in the word and a review of decoding (not guessing) strategies. If the student continues to struggle, explain how the decoding works, give the word, and have the student read the word three times. A brief definition of *bellhop* would also be in order. Finally, give words of encouragement for positive behaviors, like staying calm, working hard, and persevering, which, by the way, is a great vocabulary word to teach!

Follow this link to explore Dot and Check spelling, a nifty multi-grade instant error correction routine for spelling dictation.

Figure 5.1 An Example of Dot and Check Spelling

Systematic and Cumulative Teaching

This can be done for many subjects but here we are talking about spelling and phonics. *Systematic* means your spelling-phonics sequence begins with the most basic elements, follows a logical order, and progresses methodically to what is most complex. *Cumulative* means each step is based on concepts previously mastered.

Multi-Sensory Instruction

Because of their neurobiological differences, students with dyslexia have a difficult time recording and retrieving sound–letter associations into and from their "brain dictionary." Multi-sensory instruction activates the senses of movement and touch, thus supporting literacy learning by using brain pathways outside of the sight- and sound-based reading circuit (9, 10, 11). Through multi-sensory activities, students not only learn by reading and writing but also by singing and chanting, moving their bodies, and manipulating materials with their hands. There's no need to do this for hours at a time; very short bursts distributed throughout the day are effective. Look for the multi-sensory components in many of the upcoming activities.

Q A What phonological skills should I concentrate on when working with students with dyslexia?

Concentrate on *phonemic skills*, from segmenting and blending to deletion and manipulation.

The word *phonology* embraces many concepts and skills, including counting syllables, learning onsets and rimes, and identifying rhyming words. Phonemic skills, however, are the most important phonological skills for students to master (12, 13).

Phonemes are the discrete sounds of any language. English happens to have forty-four. Phonemic skills benefit all students; students with dyslexia may need many more repetitions to master particular ones, such as segmenting, blending, deleting, and manipulating (14, 15). One final thing: phoneme discrimination and production is not an end in and of itself. The purpose of teaching phonemic awareness is to enable a student to form the sound–letter associations of the English language. So, tie phonemes to the letters that represent them (16). Quickly and correctly recalled sound–letter associations are the ultimate goal.

Q A How much time should I devote to phonemic awareness instruction?

Give short bursts, perhaps five to seven minutes or a bit longer, and distribute the practice throughout the day and week.

Remember to keep the faith: some students might not reach benchmarks for many months, even in the face of consistent, effective instruction. As a reading specialist, I taught kindergarten intervention groups for years, working with three to four children at a time, beginning in late September. Every other day I would see a group for twenty minutes, engaging them with activities that taught phonemic awareness, letter identification, and sound–letter association. By the end of November, some children had strong phonemic skills, mastery over a dozen sound–letter associations, and could read a few CVC words. But others didn't reach this goal until late January or mid-February.

Older students who are reading well do not need phonemic instruction. But if low-achieving students in third grade and up lack sound–letter associations and phonemic awareness, give them phonemic instruction and strongly connect it to spelling. Remember, the goal is proficiency with sound–letter relationships, not stand-alone phonemic skills (17).

What activities help students develop phonemic awareness?

Many activities teach children to hear, produce, manipulate, and blend phonemes. There are many examples; here are three that I find most successful, all multi-sensory in nature.

Hear It, Say It, Tap It

For students in kindergarten and first grade, use the "board and paddle" method. Hold one arm out straight from your body. This is the "board" on which a student taps. The other hand forms the "Scout's honor" sign—your pointer, middle, and ring fingers are held out as you hold your pinky down with your thumb. This is the tapping "paddle." Say a target word, such as *slim*, and have the students repeat it. Next, tap out the sounds: /s/, /l/, /i/, /m/, moving down your arm, shoulder to wrist, tapping out each sound with your paddle. Finally, say the word again as you slide your paddle from shoulder to wrist, blending the phonemes together to make a word.

For older students, use the "finger tapping" method. Say the word, *slim*, and have the students repeat it. Using the dominant hand, tap out each phoneme by touching, in sequence, fingers to thumb. For right handed students, start with the pinky finger and move to the pointer, saying each phoneme: /s/, /l/, /i/, /m/. For left handed students, start with the pointer and move to the pinky. Blend the sounds back into a word by touching all the fingers to the thumb and saying the word.

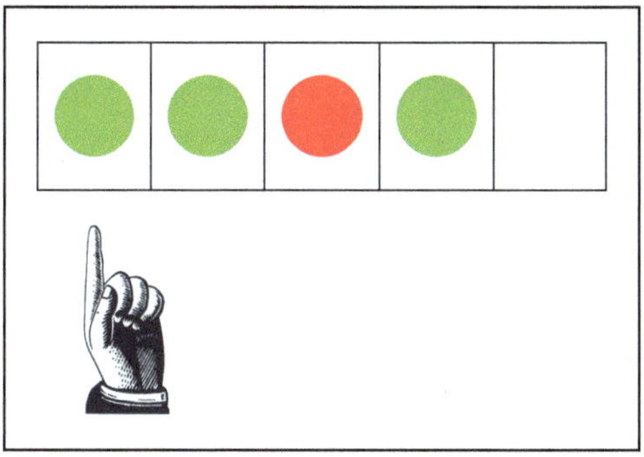

Figure 5.2 Token Push for a Four-Phoneme Word Like *Skin* or *Bent*

Token Push Using Elkonin Boxes (Sound Boxes)

In this activity, each box in a grid contains one sound (phoneme). You can use pennies but for students who have dyslexia, tokens might be best because then you can use two colors, one for consonants and another for vowels.

For a four-phoneme word like *skin*, place four tokens under a grid of four boxes (see Figure 5.2). Using the Hear It, Say It, Tap It method described earlier, tap out the phonemes and blend them back into a word. Then have your student say the phonemes as they push the tokens into the box. Finally, have your student slide their finger below the tokens and say the word again. This activity is a precursor to spelling boxes, described in the next section.

Token Pull Using Elkonin Boxes

As before, use pennies or tokens. For a four-phoneme word like *slap*, do the routine as described previously, ending with a finger slide below the tokens as the word is said. Then pull off the first token, leaving the sounds/l/, /a/, /p/. Ask, "What word is this?" or say, "Say *slap* without the/s/" (the correct response is *lap*). Other words to use include *flip* (lip), *stop* (top), and *plug* (lug).

Students should also practice deleting sounds from the ends of words. For example, pull the last token off the word *dent*, leaving the sounds/d/, /e/, /n/. Ask, "What word is this?" or say, "Say *dent* without the/t/" (the correct response is *den*). Other words to use in this activity include *lips* (lip), *tend* (ten), and *hump* (hum).

Mark Weakland Literacy YouTube channel

Visit Mark's YouTube channel, Mark Weakland Literacy, to see demonstrations of the activities given in this chapter.

What activities effectively teach sound–letter associations?

There are many activities that teach sound–letter associations, the building blocks of reading. Here are three; notice their multi-sensory aspects.

Letter Identification and Sound Association

In a 2015 *Reading Teacher* article (18), researcher, D. Ray Reutzel, proposed a twelve- to fifteen-minute letter identification lesson that simultaneously teaches upper- and lower-case letter forms and the associated phoneme. In Appendix A, you'll find an adaptation of his lesson, which can be repeated for each letter in an introductory letter sequence. If your sequence begins with *m*, *s*, *i*, *t*, *a*, *p*, and your students have mastered each sound–letter association, they can quickly move to spelling and reading VC, CVC, CVCC, and CCVC words like *it*, *at*, *sit*, *sat*, *mat*, *pat*, *pit*, *tap*, *tip*, *sap*, *sip*, *map*, *Tim*, *past*, *mast*, *mist*, *taps*, *maps*, *tips*, *spit*, and *spat*. Wow, what a lot of words!

Sound Boxes to Spelling Boxes

Spelling boxes [Figure 5.3] support students as they learn sound–letter associations. Students listen to a word, segment it into individual

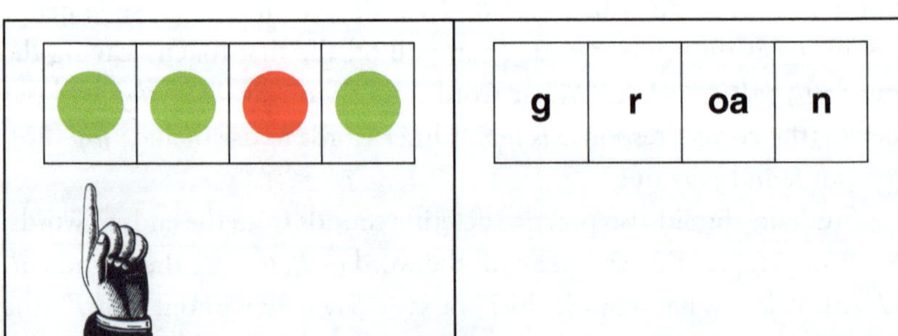

Figure 5.3 Sound Boxes Become Spelling Boxes

phonemes, and then fill in the sound boxes with the letter or letters that represent each phoneme. Last, they swipe their fingers under the letters, left to right, and read the word. In this way, students begin to master the alphabetic principle: sounds are represented by letters, letters stand for sounds.

Follow your spelling-phonic sequence as you use spelling grids. To begin, students might spell and read CVC words such as *sip*, *bat*, and *pit*. Later, students with more advanced knowledge of spelling patterns can use the same three-box grid to spell *raid*, *church*, and *thought*. Words like *raid* also give opportunities to study vocabulary.

Mapping Template

Phonology, spelling, and phonics are combined in the orthographic mapping routine Hear It, Say It, Tap It—Map It, Read It, Write It. Laminate the template located in Appendix B or place it in a plastic sleeve that works with dry erase markers. In brief, here are directions:

- Say the target word. The students repeat the word.
- Students tap out the sounds of the word by using the sound grid, one tap per box. If more support is needed, have students place tokens into the sound boxes.
- Students spell the word, filling each box of the grid that contains a sound with a written letter or letters for the phoneme.
- Students read the word by swiping their fingers along the arrow underneath the letters written in the boxes.
- Students write the word one last time on the line below and then read it.

What practices help to teach spelling-phonics to proficiency?

The path to proficiency includes practices such as these: toggling between spelling and phonics, direct and explicit instruction, repeated practice, following a systematic sequence, teaching patterns to mastery, not teaching too many patterns at once (one to two for beginners, three to four for those further along), and a sequence of phonics instruction that matches your sequence of spelling instruction.

The hyphenated term *spelling-phonics* (*sponics*!) is being used intentionally, as opposed to separated spelling and phonics. The revered

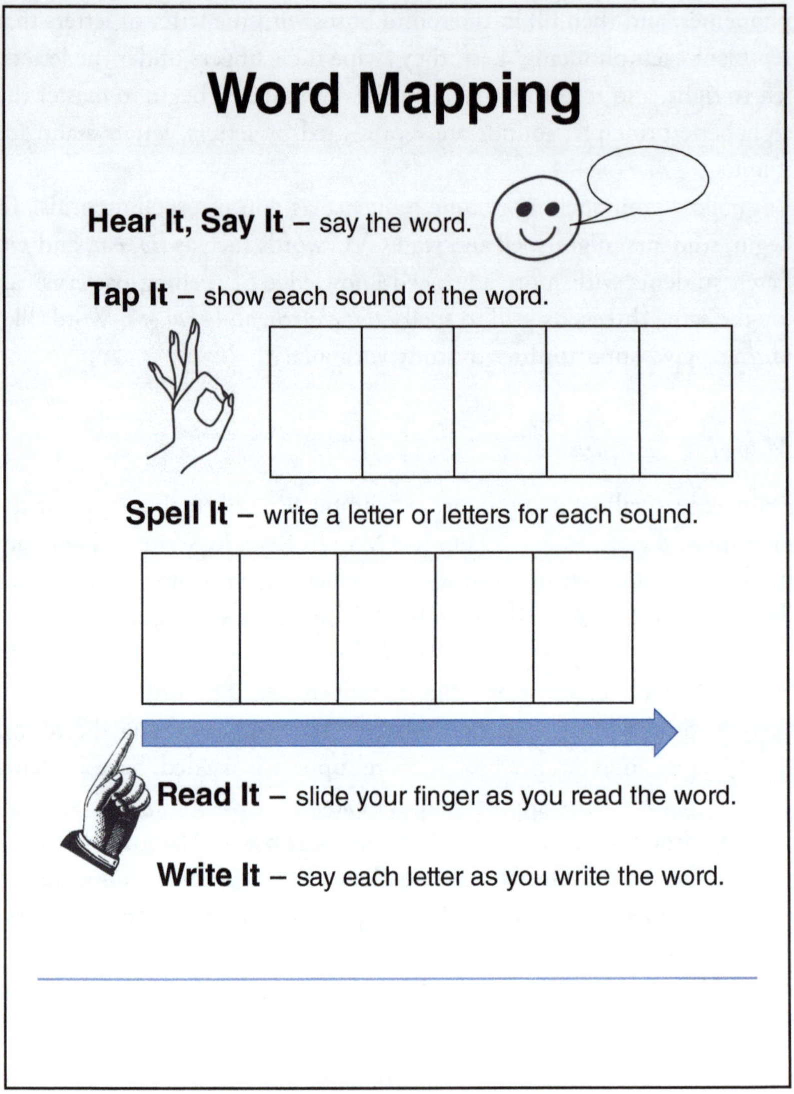

Figure 5.4 Word Mapping Template from Appendix B

reading researcher, Linnea Ehri, famously said encoding (spelling) and decoding (phonics) are "two sides of the same coin," meaning the processes are closely related and the correlation between the two is high (19). This does not mean stand-alone spelling and stand-alone phonics instruction are not appropriate. At times, some separation can be helpful. But moving back and forth between the two helps you easily give more repetitions, keep students engaged, and teach patterns to mastery. Most reading interventions for students with dyslexia have activities that toggle between spelling and phonics (20), and this book suggests general classroom teachers do the same.

Spelling with Letter Tiles

In this activity a teacher provides specific letter tiles and guides students as they spell words, providing practice for sound–letter associations that have been previously introduced. For example, when given the letter tiles *i*, *o*, *p*, *t*, *ch*, and *g*, students practice building this word sequence:

it → fit→ pit → tip → chip → chop → top → pot → got

The activity's kinesthetic nature helps wire the reading circuit, keeps kids engaged, and reduces the number of paper–pencil tasks done in a day. My favorite letter tile product is the *Magnetic Journal* from the Wilson Reading System. Of course, there are others. In my opinion, the best products:

- are strongly magnetic, with dedicated areas devoted to holding the tiles and spelling the words,
- are color coded—for example, vowels and vowel teams are one color, consonants and consonant diagraphs are another,
- are easy to manage and then store,
- present certain letter combinations as inseparable chunks because together the letters form a distinctive sound. Examples of these indivisible sound–letter chunks are *-an*, *-am*, *-all*, *-unk*, *-eigh*, *-ink*, *-tion*, and *-dge.*

To practice reading as well as spelling, have your students swipe their finger, left to right, under the word as they read it.

Word Ladders

The most basic ladders transform one word into another, one letter at a time. Each change creates a new word; each new word is a rung on the ladder. Starting at the bottom, it may take a student five or more words to reach the target word at the top. For example, here's how to change a cat into a dog:

cat → sat → sit → hit → hot → hog → dog

Basic word ladders help children notice sounds and their spellings, especially inner vowels. To change one word into another, students must listen to sounds (phonology) and decide on letters (orthography). Later, when students reach higher levels of vowel spelling complexity (as in AI, AY, OW, OA), they might change more than one letter at a time. For example, in this ladder students change more than one letter at a time:

float → *flow* → *grow* → *gray* → *grain* → *brain* → *bray*

Once the ladder is done, have your students read it from bottom to top. Then read it from top to bottom! Continue building automatic word recognition by asking the students to touch a word you say. For example: "Touch the word *flow*. Touch the word *gray*. Touch the word *brain*." Also, build vocabulary by asking them to touch the word that matches a definition. For example: "Touch a word that is the sound a donkey makes." [Students touch *bray*.]

Decodable Text

Once readers have learned a few basic sound–letter associations and can blend left to right, they are ready for decodable books (21). Rather than guessing from pictures or predicting from context clues, decodable books encourage students to sound out words using decoding strategies. If your letter teaching sequence begins with *m, a, s, i, t, g, d, o, l,* a beginning decodable book might use VC and CVC words to tell the story of Tim and Mit, giving sentences like *Tim is glad. Mit is mad. Tim got a dog. Mit got a log! Tim's dog is Dot. Sit Dot, sit!* As your spelling-phonics sequence unfolds, decodable books in a series introduce words with more complex structures, like vowel and consonant digraphs, and morphemes like *-ing* and plural *-s*.

Over the last ten years, decodable books have been published in greater numbers and with increasing quality. Many now have engaging characters, a problem-solution, and a beginning, middle, and end. There are even decodable chapter books that tell stories of mystery and adventure.

I've personally seen first- and third-grade children thoroughly enjoy decodable books, mostly because they can read them on their own! The positive reinforcement cycle these children experience is a simple but powerful one: reading success creates happiness, happiness builds motivation to read, motivation to read leads to more reading, more reading creates more reading success!

Linnea Ehri, who developed the phase theory for automatic sight word recognition and helped coin the term *orthographic mapping*, says this:

> **Orthographic mapping involves the formation of letter-sound connections to bond the spellings, pronunciations, and meanings of specific words in memory. It explains how children learn to read words by sight, to spell words from memory, and to acquire vocabulary words from print (22).**

What spelling strategies might a student with dyslexia use to help themselves?

First, a quick reminder of how the reading circuit operates.

To become fluent readers, students must perfectly and permanently store hundreds of words. These words are combinations of spelling, sound, and meaning. As a reader's eyes scan sentences during reading, words are automatically recognized. This is happening right now as you read the words in this sentence! In effect, every word is a sight word; as your eyes land on each correct letter sequence, the word's sound and meaning are automatically retrieved from your brain.

To write, a similar process occurs. As I type these words, my brain is "speaking" them in my head and retrieving their spellings. If there's a word I can't automatically spell, like the word *anaphylactic*, I employ a strategy. Typically, I sound it out and spell it as best I can (my first attempt was *anaphalactic*). Next, I employ a strategy to correct the incorrect word. For example, noticing that my MS Word application has underlined the word in red, I engage the spell check and choose one of the words given as an option. Often, I recognize the word but sometimes I simply make a best guess. This type of spelling is strategy-based.

Because storing and retrieving sight words are difficult for students with dyslexia, they need spelling strategies other than "find the correct letter sequence in your brain." The following strategies are appropriate for various ages and grade levels.

- Use a **magic line** to stand in for a word you don't know how to spell. For example, if a writer wants to say, "My dog is a Pomeranian" but doesn't know how to spell Pomeranian, they write their sentence like this: "My dog is a P________." Then, they keep writing. This is in lieu of stopping, struggling to spell the word, and possibly losing their train of thought. The magic line also lets students use their most sophisticated words, even when they can't spell them. At first, magic lines can be left entirely blank. Later, teachers can encourage students to go back to their lines and add letters that match some of the word's sounds. For example, they might write their dog's breed like this, P mra neen.
- **Circle, come back, and correct** is a strategy like the magic line. Writers spell the word to the best of their ability, circle it, and keep on writing. Later, they come back to their circled words and attempt to correct them (see next bullet).
- **Get help from a friend, handbook, and/or technology.** Using a Writer's Handbook, doing an internet search, using a spell check function, and enlisting the help of a friend are spelling strategies that dovetail nicely with the magic line and circle, come back, and correct strategies.
- **Employ a mnemonic device** (see next).

What is a mnemonic device and how can it help students with dyslexia?

A mnemonic device is a memory aid that helps someone store and then retrieve information. The trick is to associate something hard to remember with something easy to remember. What makes something easy to remember? It rhymes, is clever, has rhythm, or is fun. For example, perhaps you can't remember that E, G, B, D, and F are the five notes that fall on the staff lines of the treble clef. Well, maybe you can remember one of these catchy phrases: "**E**very **G**reat **B**ird **D**oes **F**ly" or "**E**ven **G**eorge **B**ush **D**oes **F**art."

Mnemonic devices can be used to store all types of information. In this case, students are using them to store the correct letter sequences of spelling patterns or whole words. Student-used mnemonics include 1) using a clever phrase, 2) saying a word in a funny way, 3) drawing a picture or telling a story. Here's a chart of mnemonics in action. Caution: these are *my* mnemonic devices and are not necessarily for kids!

Mnemonic Device	*Word You Want to Spell*	*Strategy in Action*
Use a clever phrase	*friend* *principal* *vacuum*	"Be a fri**end** to the **end**." "**I** am a friend to the end." "The princi**pal** is your **pal**." "You and you must vacuum the rug."
Say it in a funny way	*Wednesday* *environment* *people*	Say, "**wed** -nes -day." Say, "en -**vi**- ron-ment." Say, "pe-**o**-pl-e" (sounds like *pee-o-pull-ee*)
Tell a funny story and draw a picture	*silhouette*	 I see a silhouette of a man. He's tossing a silver coin next to a house as he smokes a cigarette.

The phonics program, *Secret Stories*, uses fun phrases, stories, and pictures to help students remember phonic patterns and make the English "code" not so secret. You too can create mnemonic devices for your students. Give them to the youngest kids and encourage older ones to devise their own (ownership makes remembering more likely). And speaking of remembering, remember this: linking instruction to a strong positive emotion, like delight or happiness, helps make learning permanent.

What classroom activities boost automatic word recognition?

Many published programs promote fluent reading, a.k.a. words read accurately, at an acceptable rate, and with expression. But you don't need a special program to run effective activities that support word recognition.

In the 1970s, Dr. J. Samuels created a formal routine that included repeatedly reading a passage with guidance from a teacher and then peers. He called the routine *guided repeated reading.* To this day, the routine is cited as an effective way to build fluency (23, 24). Briefly stated, it involves two students who coach each other. Together, they set goals and then repeatedly read a passage, each alternately acting as a coach.

Repeated Reading article from Iowa Reading Research Center

To learn the routine's specific steps and components, and to understand how and why it works, follow the link to the Iowa Reading Research Center's article.

An informal version of the routine is *I Read, We Read, You Read.* First pick a passage that is giving students some difficulty. Then, have them follow along as you read the passage accurately, at a moderate speed, and with expression (*I Read*). Next, have the students read the same passage out loud with you, reminding them to try to match your rate of speed and expression (*We Read*). Finally, have them read the passage back to you, again at a moderate rate and with expression (*You Read*).

Additional ways to promote automatic word recognition and reading fluency can be found on my YouTube channel, Mark Weakland Literacy. Check out the videos on *read to the wall* and *paintbrush reading*, among others.

Should I use only decodable text with my students who have dyslexia?

Definitely not.

One key to teaching all students to read is to get them hooked on books at a young age. Decodable readers can hook students because their decodability brings reading success early and easily. But some decodable text can be dry in tone and restricted in the topics and characters they present. So, while decodable books are a necessary part of instruction, they are in no way the only books to offer.

Quality children's literature also helps to hook students on reading. Offering a wide variety of interesting books on many reading levels is key.

So is providing reading in shared, small group, and independent settings. Using quality children's literature during shared reading (as in an interactive read aloud) is relatively easy. Creating effective independent reading routines that make use of a well-stocked classroom library takes a bit more work. But it is well worth the effort, because independent reading builds the background and vocabulary knowledge readers need to enjoy the books they'll read in the future (25). In effect, the rich get richer.

For students who may not like to read, try any or all of the following ideas. My mother, who was masterful at running independent reading routines, would exclaim to her students, day after day, "Let's read, read, read!"

- Create a culture of reading by promoting books, highlighting books, and generally having enthusiasm for books.
- Carve out time for students to buddy read, share their thoughts and ideas on books, practice a book passage and share it with peers, etc.
- Create a culture of writing by promoting professional writers, discussing writing topics, using elements of the Writer's Workshop model, and teaching students how to write well about topics of their choice. Also, give students time to read their writing to others.
- Use classroom structures and routines like the "I Can" list or "Must Do, May Do" list, both of which help teachers and students manage independent reading and writing time. An "I Can" poster lists the activities students can choose to do during independent reading and writing time, such as "I can re-read my decodable book, I can partner read a buddy book, I can write on a topic of my choice." Meanwhile, a "Must Do, May Do" list is akin to the Premack Principle (or Grandma's Rule), whereby a student must do a less-preferred teacher directed activity first, such as re-read your decodable text or practice your sight words, before they choose a preferred activity of their choice, such as reading with a buddy or writing and illustrating a story.
- Include hi-lo books and graphic novels in your classroom library. Both hi-lo books and graphic novels engage reluctant readers—hi-lo books through their high-interest topics coupled with easier-to-read sentences, and graphic novels through their wealth of amazing illustrations coupled with fewer words, often presented in appealing dialogue.

- Try some poetry. Many poems use rhyming patterns, higher level vocabulary, figurative language, and clever storytelling. Best of all, poems are short and can be less intimidating to students who don't like to read. Carve out time at the end of the month for students to read or perform a poem. Have a poetry slam.
- Build a well-stocked classroom library organized in unleveled book bins and front-facing book displays. Include many genres, levels, subjects, and books with diverse characters that reflect the lives of your students.
- Structure your program so there's at least a twenty-minute block of time, every day, for independent reading and writing.

While these ideas are important for every elementary grade, they are probably most effective when done in the early grades. In the end, simultaneously teaching decoding to mastery and giving access to rich literature helps to prevent the large "reading practice gaps" that can develop in older readers with weak reading skills (26).

There is a fairly strong case to be made for putting more emphasis on *text reading during reading intervention time* (27, 28). This means that rather than focusing solely on encoding and decoding practiced through word lists, isolated sentences, and short decodable paragraphs, it is beneficial to also have students read longer, more authentic paragraphs and even books. Why? Reading articles and books increases a student's exposure to a variety of real-world sentences and paragraphs.

What is structured literacy, and should I use it to teach my students who have dyslexia?

Structured literacy is a combination of teaching techniques and content emphasis. The techniques and content have been around for decades but the term was coined by the International Dyslexia Association in 2014. According to the IDA, while the ineffective methodology known as *whole language* had a catchy name, the body of effective practice that included explicitly and systematically taught phonological awareness and phonics did not (29). Rather, there were only program names, like Sonday, Wilson, and Orton-Gillingham. And so, the IDA created a single, memorable name—structured literacy.

Structured literacy, which grounds instruction firmly in science (30), is defined in a dozen different ways by a dozen different organizations. Here's my take on it:

***What* (content to teach)**	***How* (to teach the content)**
1 Phonology 2 Sound–symbol association 3 Phonics and spelling, including syllables 4 Morphology 5 Semantics These content areas put an emphasis on language structures.	1 Systematic 2 Explicit and direct 3 To mastery 4 Cumulative 5 Diagnostic 6 With corrective feedback

Over time, more literacy components have come to rest under structured literacy's umbrella. For me, the most recently added elements boil down to *comprehension* and *writing*. When you survey the literature, however, you'll see a variety of terms, including *text composition*, *text comprehension*, *written expression*, *vocabulary*, *language knowledge*, and *reading comprehension*.

Certainly, every practice that is now a part of structured literacy should be used to teach students with dyslexia. But I would suggest two things. First, keep formative assessment firmly in sight. The question is always, what does this student need? Second, pay special attention to structured literacy's original formulation (shown in the chart). Why? This version directly addresses the core weaknesses of most students who have dyslexia, namely deficits in phonological skills, decoding, and spelling (31).

When phonics instruction has an initial focus on small sound–letter relationships (as opposed to instruction that focuses on larger units), it seems to lead to better reading outcomes for all children (32). Therefore, structured literacy is a starting point for *all* students in your classroom!

Will students who have dyslexia ever become quick readers or excellent spellers?

Possibly.

When it comes to reading words, the goal is high accuracy and at least a moderate amount of speed. With proper instruction, some students experience a breakthrough and make large gains in reading rates. The reading speeds of others may edge up slowly over time and in small increments. In the end, some students may always be slow and steady readers. This is fine, as long as they read with a high degree of accuracy (which is linked to comprehension) and enough speed to move them through the material they need to learn (volume is also linked to comprehension). Reading rate becomes more important in the upper grades, where large amounts of information must be digested. But then, technology can be brought to bear if needed (see the next chapter).

As for spelling, some people will simply never be strong spellers. Fortunately, there are a plethora of strategies for dealing with inaccurate spelling. It behooves teachers to first teach self-monitoring, as in "I think some of the words I just wrote are misspelled." Once misspelled words are identified, other strategies come into play, like using a writer's handbook or a word processor's *editor* function.

Should I focus on comprehension skills with students who are dyslexic?

Yes but…

Comprehension of text is the goal of reading. Full stop. When a reader "reads" with little to no understanding, they are simply calling out words. A few children (sometimes labeled *hyperlexic*) are wonders at automatically recognizing words but fail to understand such things as the plot, character emotions, figurative language, and connections between events (33).

Students who have dyslexia are in some ways the opposite of hyperlexic readers. Their oral language comprehension, ability to make connections, and capacity to understand emotions are often strong. What limits their ability to understand text is their difficulty with decoding and word finding; because they can't read the words, they can't understand them, and when they give most of their energy and attention to decoding, they have little left over for deciphering meaning. So, to boost their automatic word recognition, classroom instruction typically focuses on phonology, phonics, spelling, and fluency.

The caveat is that until students with dyslexia reach some semblance of fluency, they encounter a limited number of words. This inhibits the growth of the vocabulary and world knowledge they need to further comprehend text. Thus, students who have dyslexia *will* need comprehension instruction that builds vocabulary, background knowledge, and the use of meta-cognition strategies.

All students need comprehension instruction! In the end, the amount each gets depends upon the need. To decide what to teach, look to your formative and benchmark assessment scores, and stay in touch with your "teacher sense."

In my classroom, how much time should I devote to each component of literacy?

This question has no specific answer. There is little research evidence to support any exact amount of time that should be given to any specific component of reading or writing, from phonology and phonics to spelling, grammar, and sentence structure (34). Also, students have differing profiles of strengths and needs. Thus, the type and amount of instruction each student needs to acquire skills and information will vary, sometimes greatly.

Still, every day teachers face practical issues that demand action and so, in this book's Appendix C are sample lesson plans. Each provides a possible structure (there are many) for a lesson a student with dyslexia might need.

Do interventions like colored overlays and special fonts help people with dyslexia learn to read and spell?

A few say yes, most say no.

The foundational literacy skills that lead to fluent reading are built from instruction *based in print*, such as pairing sound and print to teach sound–letter associations (35). In other words, interventions *not* based on print but claiming to remediate or "treat" dyslexia are not effective. Ineffective interventions include the following:

Balancing exercises, fish-oils, medications that improve the inner ear, etc.	According to the Dyslexia Help website (University of Michigan), there is *no* validated research to support the idea that any of the following help students overcome their dyslexia: "... special balancing exercises, fish-oils, glasses with tinted lenses... modeling clay letters, inner-ear-improving medications, training primitive reflexes, eye occlusion (patching), etc." (36) Certainly, some of these things can produce health benefits for anyone needing to boost their omega-3 levels (through fish oil), improve their balance (through balancing exercises), cure an inner ear infection (through medication), and so forth. But none of this has anything to do with dyslexia!

(Continued)

Specialized fonts; dyslexia fonts	Researchers have found that a specialized "dyslexia font" neither helps nor hinders readers any more than a "normal" font does. Also, studies show a dyslexia font was not preferred by most students (37). On the other hand, and on a personal note, I have met two teachers with dyslexia who told me a dyslexia font makes reading much easier for them.
Vision therapy	Examples of *unsupported* dyslexia therapies that involve vision include visual training, muscle exercises, and eye-tracking exercises (38). Again, dyslexia does not flow from visual problems. Rather, it flows from neurodiversity. Still, some reading difficulties can be caused by vision problems and so one can also not say vision therapy cannot correct a reading problem. It's important to remember the therapy must be aligned with the cause.
Colored overlays	Because dyslexia is not connected to visual difficulties, colored overlays for text are not effective tools for boosting learning when it comes to reading and spelling (39). Some studies posit that any helpful effects are the result of the placebo effect (40). This is interesting to think about. For example, positive effects could be due to general stress reduction. Because reading is difficult (stressful) for someone with dyslexia, changing from white paper to a perceived "soothing color" of yellow or blue may give some psychological relief.

If my student with dyslexia needs a specialized program, which one is best?

For students who struggle to learn how to read, a structured literacy approach in a general education classroom is more effective than any approach that emphasizes leveled readers and the three-cuing system, gives overly broad spelling instruction, underutilizes explicit instruction, doesn't emphasize the mastering of sound–letter relationships, and so forth.

But what *specific* structured literacy program is best? There is no magic wand or silver bullet. This is especially thought provoking because interventions like Orton-Gillingham are "firmly entrenched in policy and practice" even though there is "limited evidence supporting their use" (41). When it comes to remediating either a specific labeled reading difficulty, such as dyslexia, or a general difficulty, such as a lack of fluency or dearth of reading comprehension, Dr. Louise Spear-Swerling clearly says there is no empirical evidence that identifies "one particular Structured Literacy program or method as more effective than all others." Spear-Swerling goes on to say, "… the limited evidence on many specific details of intervention design and delivery argue against an unyielding reliance on one particular program or method" (42).

Still, while reading experts make a case against any one program or method, there are many programs that incorporate *practices* proven to be effective at teaching foundational reading skills. And teachers and districts must choose something! The following is a partial list of programs used in some schools and districts. A final decision on which program to choose will most likely be dictated by factors such as cost, training availability, personal preference, the demographics of the school, and the knowledge district administrators have about all things literacy.

- *Orton-Gillingham.* The program creators pioneered a combination of explicitly teaching the connections between letters and sounds, with multi-sensory teaching and systematic, sequential lessons.
- The spirit of OG permeates many programs created over the decades. Examples include:
  - *Barton System: Reading and Spelling*, created by Susan Barton.
  - *Wilson Reading System*, created by Barbara Wilson.
  - *Sonday System*, created by (you guessed it) Arlene and Karen Sonday.
- Newer structured programs are popping up everywhere, including in the Pacific Northwest (Laura Rogen with *Wired for Reading* and *Word Wires*), the Midwest (Marsha Geller, Beth Hatlen, and Karla O'Brien with the *SLANT System*), and the Central South (the folks at Texas Educational Service Center 4 with *Reading by Design*).

The abstract of a 2021 *meta-analysis* of the effectiveness of Orton-Gillingham reading interventions for students with word-level reading disabilities said evidence from prior analyses, the What Works Clearinghouse, and the meta-analysis itself did *not* find definitive evidence that Orton-Gillingham interventions significantly improve foundational skill outcomes for students with dyslexia (43). The study went on to say that while OG interventions "may hold promise for positively impacting this population of students," more research is needed.

***

To summarize, this chapter described effective teaching techniques, phonological activities that emphasize phonemic awareness and help children learn sound–letter associations, spelling-phonic activities that help students master encoding and decoding patterns and automatically recognize words, and fluency activities that build accuracy and can also boost word reading rates. This chapter also defined structured literacy, listed classroom practices that are *not* supported by research, and discussed programs specifically designed for students with dyslexia. Whew!

One big idea to take away from all of this is that a general education teacher can do a lot to help students with dyslexia master reading, writing, and spelling. Help doesn't come from only Tier II and III reading interventions. Rather, help comes when students with dyslexia are taught within a strongly integrated multi-tiered system in which all teachers are pulling in the same direction with great expertise. Here's another big idea to take away: when effective practices like direct and explicit instruction and well-run independent reading and writing routines are employed, the practices benefit *all* children in a classroom.

In the last chapter, we'll look at how we can help students who have developed anxiety, a poor self-image, and reading avoidance behaviors. The bad news is that many children don't understand why reading is so hard for them, don't understand their dyslexia, and frequently compare themselves to other students who are making progress easily. The good news is that a classroom teacher can do things that make school life easier and less stressful for students with dyslexia, including providing accommodations and classroom modifications that give access and comfort in a text-based world.

End of Chapter Resources

1 Kilpatrick, David. 2015. *The Essentials of Assessing, Preventing, and Overcoming Reading Difficulties.* Hoboken, NJ: Wiley & Sons, p. 271.

2 Gentry, Richard, and Gene Oullette. 2019. *Brain Words: How the Science of Reading Informs Teaching.* Portsmouth, NH: Stenhouse Publishing, p. 137.

3 Benjamin, Aaron, and Jonathan Tullis. 2010. "What Makes Distributed Practice Effective?" *Cognitive Psychology* 61 (3): 228–247.

4 Sandman-Hurley, Kelli. 2024. "Dyslexia and the English Learner Dilemma." Language. www.languagemagazine.com/dyslexia-and-the-english-learner-dilemma/#:~:text=Fluency%20and%20orthography%20issues%20are,it%20is%20an%20opaque%20language.

5 Rodrigo, Mercedes, et al. 2004. "Assessment of Orthographical Processing in Spanish Children with Dyslexia: The Role of Lexical and Sublexical Units." *Electronic Journal of Research in Educational Psychology* 2 (4).

6 Sandman-Hurley, Kelli. 2024. "Dyslexia and the English Learner Dilemma." Language. www.languagemagazine.com/dyslexia-and-the-english-learner-dilemma/#:~:text=Fluency%20and%20orthography%20issues%20are,it%20is%20an%20opaque%20language.

7 Samuels, S. Jay., and Yi-Chen Wu. 2003. "*The Effects of Immediate Feedback on Reading Achievement.*" Department of Educational Psychology, University of Minnesota. http://testmaker.if-at.com/home/articles/file/research/immediate_feedback.pdf.

8 Stenger, Marianne. 2014. "Five Research-Based Tips for Providing Students with Meaningful Feedback." Edutopia. www.edutopia.org/blog/tips-providing-students-meaningful-feedback-marianne-stenger.

9 Hazaymeh, Wafa, et al. 2025. "Exploring the Efficacy of Multisensory Techniques in Enhancing Reading Fluency for Dyslexic English Language Learners." *World Journal of English Language* 15 (1): 146–159.

10 Obaid, Majeda. 2013. "The Impact of Using Multi-Sensory Approach For Teaching Students With Learning Disabilities." *Journal of International Education Research* 9 (1): 75–82.

11 Department of Physiology, Anatomy & Genetics. 2023. "Researchers Discover Why Multisensory Learning Is Beneficial For Memory." University of Oxford. www.dpag.ox.ac.uk/news/researchers-discover-why-multisensory-learning-is-beneficial-for-memory.

12 Phillips, Beth, and Shayne Piasta. 2013. "Phonological Awareness and Alphabet Knowledge: Key Precursors and Instructional Targets to Promote Reading Success." In *Early Childhood Literacy: The National Early Literacy Panel and Beyond*, ed. Timothy Shanahan and C. J. Lonigan. Baltimore, MD: Paul H. Brookes.

13 Ehri, Linnea. 1998. "Grapheme-Phoneme Knowledge Is Essential For Learning to Read Words in English." In *Word Recognition in Beginning Literacy*, ed. Jamie Metsala and Linnea Ehri. New York: Routledge.

14 Reutzel, D. Ray. 2015. "Early Literacy Research: Findings Primary-Grade Teachers Will Want to Know." *The Reading Teacher* 69 (1): 14–24.

15 Kilpatrick, David. 2015. *The Essentials of Assessing, Preventing, and Overcoming Reading Difficulties*. Hoboken, NJ: Wiley & Sons, p. 179.

16 Seidenberg, Mark. 2024. "The Phonemic Awareness Discussion." Reading Matters. https://seidenbergreading.net/author/markseidenberg/.

17 Seidenberg, Mark. 2024. "The Phonemic Awareness Discussion." Reading Matters. https://seidenbergreading.net/author/markseidenberg/.

18 Reutzel, D. Ray. 2015. "Early Literacy Research: Findings Primary-Grade Teachers Will Want to Know." *The Reading Teacher* 69 (1): 14–24.

19 Ehri, Linnea. 2000. "Learning to Read and Learning to Spell: Two Sides of a Coin." *Topics in Language Disorder* 20 (3): 19–36.

20 Woolridge, Lorna. 2024. "The Big Five: Phonics–Orthographic Mapping." Orton-Gillingham Online Academy. https://ortongillinghamonlinetutor.com/the-big-five-phonics-orthographic-mapping/.

21 Reading Rockets. 2024. "What Are Decodable Books and Why Are They Important?" Reading Rockets. www.readingrockets.org/topics/curriculum-and-instruction/articles/what-are-decodable-books-and-why-are-they-important.

22 Ehri, Linnea. 2014. "Orthographic Mapping in the Acquisition of Sight Word Reading, Spelling, Memory, and Vocabulary Learning." *Scientific Studies of Reading* 18 (1): 5–21, p. 5.

23 Iowa Reading Research Center. 2019. "Repeated Reading with Goal Setting for Reading Fluency: Focusing on Reading Quality Rather Than Reading Speed." Iowa Reading Research Center. https://irrc.education.uiowa.edu/blog/2019/02/repeated-reading-goal-setting-reading-fluency-focusing-reading-quality-rather-reading.

24 Samuels, S. Jay. 1979. "The Method of Repeated Readings." *The Reading Teacher* 32 (4): 403–408. www.jstor.org/stable/20194790.

25 Liu, Jiren, and Jainling Zhang. 2018. "The Effects of Extensive Reading on English Vocabulary Learning: A Meta-Analysis."

English Language Teaching 11 (6): 1–15. http://doi.org/10.5539/elt.v11n6p1.

26 Torgesen, Joseph. 2004. "Lessons Learned From Research on Interventions For Students Who Have Difficulty Learning to Read." In *The Voice of Evidence in Reading Research*, ed. Peggy McCardle and Vinita Chhabra. Baltimore, MD: Brookes Publishing Co.

27 Institute of Education Sciences. 2016. "Foundational Skills to Support Reading for Understanding in Kindergarten Through 3rd Grade." U.S. Department of Education. Available at https://ies.ed.gov/ncee/WWC/Docs/PracticeGuide/wwc_foundationalreading_040717.pdf.

28 Kilpatrick, David. 2015. *The Essentials of Assessing, Preventing, and Overcoming Reading Difficulties.* Hoboken, NJ: Wiley & Sons.

29 International Dyslexia Association. 2024. "What is Structured Literacy?" International Dyslexia Association. https://va.dyslexiaida.org/what-is-structured-literacy/#:~:text=When%20the%20term%20structured%20literacy,%2C%20Sonday%2C%20and%20so%20on.

30 Spear-Swerling, Louise, et al. 2021. "Structured Literacy Brief." International Dyslexia Association. https://app.box.com/s/mvuvhel6qaj8tghvu1nl75i0ndnlp0yz.

31 Spear-Swerling, Louise. 2018. "Structured Literacy and Typical Literacy Practices: Understanding Differences to Create Instructional Opportunities." *Teaching Exceptional Children* 51 (3): 201–211. https://doi.org/10.1177/0040059917750160.

32 Brady, Susan. 2011. "Efficacy of Phonics Teaching For Reading Outcomes: Indications From Post-NRP Research." In *Explaining Individual Differences In Reading: Theory and Evidence*, ed. Susan Brady, David Braze, and Carol Fowler. New York: Psychology Press.

33 Nation, Kate. 1999. "Reading Skills in Hyperlexia: A Developmental Perspective." *Psychology Bulletin* 125 (3): 338–355.

34 Spear-Swerling, Louise, et al. 2021. "Structured Literacy Brief." International Dyslexia Association. https://app.box.com/s/mvuvhel6qaj8tghvu1nl75i0ndnlp0yz.

35 Texas State Board of Education. 2024. "The Dyslexia Handbook: Procedures Concerning Dyslexia and Related Disorders." Texas State Board of Education. https://tea.texas.gov/academics/special-student-populations/special-education/texas-dyslexia-handbook.pdf.

36 Dyslexia Help. 2024. "Debunking the Myths About Dyslexia." University of Michigan. https://dyslexiahelp.umich.edu/parents/learn-about-dyslexia/what-is-dyslexia/debunking-common-myths-about-dyslexia#:~:text=Myth%3A%20Intelligence%20and%20ability%20to,%2C%20middle%2C%20or%20low%20IQ's.
37 Kuster, Susan, et al. 2018. "Dyslexie Font Does Not Benefit Reading In Children With Or Without Dyslexia." *Annals of Dyslexia* 68 (1): 25–42.
38 Handler, Sheryl, et al. 2011. "Joint Technical Report—Learning Disabilities, Dyslexia, and Vision." *Pediatrics*. https://pubmed.ncbi.nlm.nih.gov/21357342/.
39 Griffiths, Phillp, et al. 2016. "The Effect of Colored Overlays and Lenses on Reading: A Systematic Review of the Literature." *Ophthalmic & Physiological Optics* 36 (5): 519–544.
40 Griffiths, Phillp, et al. 2016. "The Effect of Colored Overlays and Lenses on Reading: A Systematic Review of the Literature." *Ophthalmic & Physiological Optics* 36 (5): 519–544.
41 Stevens, Elizabeth, et al. 2021. "Current State of the Evidence: Examining the Effects of Orton-Gillingham Reading Interventions for Students With or at Risk for Word-Level Reading Disabilities." *Exceptional Children* 87 (4): 397–417. https://pmc.ncbi.nlm.nih.gov/articles/PMC8497161/#S19.
42 Spear-Swerling, Louise, et al. 2021. "Structured Literacy Brief." International Dyslexia Association. https://app.box.com/s/mvuvhel6qaj8tghvu1nl75i0ndnlp0yz.
43 Stevens, Elizabeth, et al. 2021. "Current State of the Evidence: Examining the Effects of Orton-Gillingham Reading Interventions for Students with or at Risk for Word-Level Reading Disabilities." *Exceptional Children*. https://pmc.ncbi.nlm.nih.gov/articles/PMC8497161/pdf/nihms-1744428.pdf.

CHAPTER 6

Lowering the Stress Levels for Students with Dyslexia

Learning theory tells us that negative emotions—fear, sadness, boredom—can inhibit a student's ability to learn skills and retain information (1). Thus, teachers strive to create classroom environments that simultaneously increase positive emotions and decrease negative ones. One universal way to boost positive feelings is to set kids up to be successful in their learning. *Accommodations* and *modifications* can help in these efforts.

Accommodations provide support by changing *how* a student with a learning disadvantage, disability, or difference accesses the content all students are learning (2). Information, goals, and grading remain constant. What changes is how the content is taught, how mastery is tested, and how students interact with materials and physical spaces as they learn (3). Examples of accommodations include giving some students a text-to-speech reader and allowing others to take a test in a study carrel.

A modification, meanwhile, changes *what* a student learns (4). Modifications typically involve alterations to curriculum, assignments, goals and expectations, as well as the grading scales and test formats that assess what has been changed (5). Examples of modifications include giving a student with dyslexia two spelling patterns (*ai* and *ay*) to focus on instead of four (*a, ai, ay, eigh*) and then testing those two patterns using a fifteen-word list rather than a twenty-five-word list.

Any challenging task can be frustrating and fear producing. But when the task is learning how to read—an undertaking that takes years to accomplish under the best of circumstances—and a reading difficulty is severe, a student's emotions can become intense. Put yourself in a student's shoes and it's not hard to imagine why—most of the kids around you are learning to read quite easily (or are already fluent readers) but you are not. Adding insult to injury, your learning difficulties don't seem to go away. What's more, you are regularly expected to participate in activities that are difficult for you, day after day, month after month. Perhaps some of you don't need to imagine this terrible situation because you have lived it, as a person with dyslexia.

This chapter looks at ways of empathizing with students who have dyslexia, as well as how to implement accommodations and modifications that provide access and comfort in a text-based world. As you read, you'll notice that many of the adjustments can be offered to students without dyslexia who have similar needs, and sometimes a generally applied classroom change (like installing sound-reduction devices) will benefit every student. Putting changes into place is a balancing act, between what you can reasonably do as a teacher and what students must have to gain access to learning, but ultimately these changes are worthy of consideration because learning always happens best in a low stress, accommodating environment (6).

How can I make students with dyslexia feel more comfortable and accepted in my classroom?

You can begin by acknowledging their difficulties and demonstrating an understanding of their condition.

For students who have not been formally identified with dyslexia, it is strongly recommended that you don't try to diagnose them or suggest in any way that they have a disability. Rather, simply share your observations. Students often feel appreciative when someone cares enough to notice their learning challenges and honestly talks to them about their struggles. For example, you can tell students you understand that reading is difficult for them and that they are not alone in this difficulty—many students have a hard time learning to read. You can also explicitly explain what you will do to help them become better readers, writers, and spellers. Finally, you can recognize their strengths and describe how these strengths positively contribute to your classroom.

For students who *have* a diagnosis of dyslexia, differences in their age and background can affect their understanding of their condition and what it means to them. Thus, you'll need to be flexible in how you talk to them about their situation. Also, remember that our field's understanding and description of any given disability changes over time. For example, President Barak Obama signed legislation in 2010 that changed the label *mentally retarded* to *intellectually disabled* (7). So, do your best to stay curious and open-minded. And consider the following ideas:

- Show your students that you understand what dyslexia is.
- Invite students to talk with you about their dyslexia and their feelings around it.
- Acknowledge that you see the results of their dyslexia; tell them what you observe.
- When you see them doing specific things to overcome their difficulties (such as working hard and/or employing strategies), point them out and be supportive of their efforts.
- Finally, highlight and celebrate the strengths they have. There may be elements of literacy that these students excel in (such as making connections or understanding figurative language) and certainly they will have gifts and strong suits in areas beyond reading.

Should I help my students with dyslexia develop self-advocacy skills?

Absolutely.

Because dyslexia is rooted in biology, it is a lifelong condition. Even when many reading difficulties are overcome through effective instruction, others will continue to manifest throughout a person's life, especially when that person enters more difficult reading situations, such as starting college studies or taking on an adult job.

Over time, every person develops a stance toward the reading world. But most of us are unconscious of our viewpoint and attitude because reading is easy for us. Having dyslexia, however, necessitates a different stance, a conscious one that involves, among other things, embracing self-advocacy. As dyslexia researcher Dr. Guinevere Eden says, "… it's important for people [with dyslexia] to tell their teachers what is helpful to them, to their learning. And they need to advocate for themselves…" (8). Developing self-advocacy involves acquiring self-knowledge. A student's arc of development might include coming to understand what dyslexia is, knowing what it means for them, realizing that many people around them may not understand their situation, and finally, identifying what they themselves can do to 1) inform others and 2) get the literacy supports they need (9).

As you come to know and understand your students with dyslexia, you'll be able to help them gain agency and ownership. Talk with them about how you can play a part in not only helping them to read and write but also to navigate the greater world (which requires reading and writing skills). Discuss how positive and negative feelings can arise from dyslexia, help your students identify and play to their strengths, and discuss the modifications and adaptations that can be employed to make their journey through the reading world more positive and enjoyable.

Should I adapt my classroom's physical space to support students with dyslexia?

Yes.

For any student, a classroom that supports focus, attention, and engagement is helpful. Carefully chosen and utilized teaching techniques, materials, and curriculum can certainly help students attend. So can the set-up of the physical space in which they are learning. To this end, do your best to provide places in your room that block out at least some noise and movement. A study carrel or two can help. So can a cardboard shield and set of ear mufflers or headphones. A teacher in a seminar once told me she cleaned out a materials closet so students could sit inside the closet and work (she propped the door open, of course). Even a bit of carpeting helps bring down the sound level in a classroom, as do sliced tennis balls that cover the metal feet of chairs.

Speaking of chairs, consider healthier seating options for everyone. Can you offer seating other than four-legged chairs at desks? Also, think about the light in your classroom. Is it possible to diminish harsh fluorescent lighting and boost natural light? If students with dyslexia also happen to be uncomfortable in traditional seating and/or bothered by fluorescent lighting, as some students are, they experience additional stress above and beyond what's caused by a reading difficulty (10). Therefore, anything that can be done to diminish stress caused by other classroom issues is helpful. Finally, some students with dyslexia may have difficulty focusing. Consider placing these students closer to you and farther from distractions like a noisy heating and cooling system.

Should I adapt the written information I give to students with dyslexia?

Most likely.

It would be inaccurate to say *all* students with dyslexia need written information accommodations. But many will. Please note that the following list embraces accommodations for all types of writing (or text), from worksheets with directions to chapters in a textbook.

- **Simplify written directions**. Underline or highlight the most important parts of the directions or rewrite directions in a less wordy way. Here is an example of each:
  - "Read each sentence in the story's paragraph below. Look for words that describe the setting of the story. Underline these words and then write them in the box below the paragraph."
  - "Read the sentences. Find words that describe the setting. Underline the setting words."
- **Highlight specific parts of a text**, such as the sentence or passage that is at the core of what you want students to know or consider.
- **Read the directions out loud**, instead of asking students to read the directions to themselves.
- **Use an audio recorder**. A digital device can record your reading of written material, from directions to stories. Many recorders are inexpensive yet powerful; a quick internet search revealed two that cost $20 with 16 GB of memory. Once the information is recorded, a student can replay the recording to clarify their understanding of directions or concepts. Also, they can read the printed words silently as the recording plays and thereby practice their reading.
- **Give a cover sheet or cover card**. Some students might need a card that only covers the words below the sentence being read. Others might do best with a card that's like a window and covers words both before and after the sentence that's being read.

- **Develop and give reading guides**. For classes or subjects that involve a large amount of reading, provide a guide that explicitly states the main ideas of the text, outlines the details associated with the main ideas, and infuses questions that help keep the reader engaged. A reading guide can take some time to develop so consider working with other teachers. Divvy up the work, share with each other, and create a file that collects all the guides in one place.
- **Present smaller amounts of work**. For example, break a large assignment into smaller pieces. Provide encouragement when each small section is completed. Or simply assign less reading (because it takes longer to read text).
- **Allow the use of assistive technology**, for example an app that reads text to a student. See the upcoming sections for more details.

How can I modify my classroom library for students who have dyslexia?

Two suggestions are 1) infuse hi-lo readers and graphic novels into your library and 2) organize your books in unleveled browsing bins categorized by some sort of theme.

Hi-lo Readers

If your class regularly engages in independent reading time (and hopefully it does), stock your classroom library with some hi-lo readers, like those from High Noon, Saddleback, or Black Rabbit Books. Short for high-interest, low-readability, hi-lo readers present engaging subjects in formats that use fewer words, more white space, and less complex sentence structures. Hi-lo books often come in a series.

Graphic Novels

Like hi-lo readers, graphic novels present lots of information using fewer words, giving struggling readers another way to build their reading confidence and foster their appreciation of story. Graphic novels come in a wide variety of genres; including nonfiction books that build a reader's understanding of everything from Greek Mythology to Shakespeare.

Unleveled Book Bins Loosely Arranged By Themes

A student's interest in a topic drives their motivation to read more than the reading level of the book they have chosen (11, 12, 13). Also, low-achieving students may not want their peers to see them pulling a book from a bin marked with a low reading level. You can tackle both issues—motivation and embarrassment—by arranging your classroom library in unleveled bins categorized by themes.

Themes can be broad (nature, humor, sports, adventure) or narrow (mammals, basketball, author Dav Pilkey, the I Survived series). Once your themes are in place, be creative about how to build a wide range of levels in one bin. *The Cat in the Hat* can go in the mammals bin, a hi-lo reader about basketball records can go in the sports bin. Browsing bins with a wide range of reading levels work for all readers—sometimes accomplished readers want to relax by reading an interesting book that's easy for them to read and students who struggle may want to tackle a difficult book because the topic is so darn interesting!

Q A Is there technology that can help students with dyslexia?

Yes, there has never been more.

From audio books and voice recognition programs to the digital recorders mentioned previously, there are a plethora of technologies that help students with dyslexia access information and overcome challenges such as slow rates of reading.

Popular web browsers, such as *Chrome* and *Firefox*, have extensions that read aloud any opened website. Meanwhile, Apple devices have *Voice Over* and *Spoken Content* that reads text (in Word documents and PDFs) out loud as it highlights the words, allowing a student to read along. Popular electronic tablets, such as the *iPad Mini* and *Kindle*, also have text-to-speech and the synthetic voices are of high quality. Many of the text-to-speech apps interface with *Bookshare* and *Learning Ally*, services that provide e-books to people with disabilities.

Conversely, there are speech-to-print programs, like *Dragon Naturally Speaking*. These apps generate text for any assignment typically handwritten or typed, such as answers to homework questions, stories written during Writing Workshop time, essays for subject area classes, and so on.

Recording devices, whether dedicated digital recorders or a voice memo app on a phone or smart tablet, let students record their oral reading. They can then play back the recording and analyze their accuracy, phrasing, and expression.

Finally, devices like Apple's iPad support dozens of learning apps that help teachers provide repetition that builds skills in engaging ways. For example, there is *ABC Writing*, for struggling readers who need word pattern practice. From a large library of basic words, the app spells a word letter-by-letter, reads the whole word, and gives students the opportunity to practice writing the word by tracing over it.

Obviously, the world of tech is constantly changing, with new products out every year. So, keep your eyes open for upgrades listed on sites like *PC Magazine*, as well as the assistive technology pages of long-standing sites like *The International Dyslexia Association* and *The Yale Center for Dyslexia and Creativity*. Another suggestion is to make friends with the assistive tech consultants who work for your state's educational support organization, such as the Intermediate Units (IUs) of Pennsylvania, the Boards of Cooperative Educational Services (BOCES) of New York, and the Education Service Centers (ESCs) of Texas. Assistive tech consultants are a wealth of information and often provide free training and technical assistance to teachers in public school systems.

What about note taking? Should I ask a student with dyslexia to take notes?

For students with dyslexia, consider alternatives to traditional note taking. This is a variation on the previously mentioned "allow students to report out in ways other than writing." Alternatives include the following:

- Give a copy of the lecture notes. Even better, give a summarized outline of the lecture that contains fewer words. The student follows along as the teacher lectures and then re-reads the notes at home.
- Allow the use of assistive tech, whereby the student uses a device and app to turn a spoken lecture into a printed text. The notes are then re-read by a peer or someone at home. Or an app can reverse the process, reading the transcribed words out loud.
- Allow the student to do Sketch Notes. This accommodation involves giving a student a T-chart. As the teacher talks, the student takes notes in pictorial form on the left side of the chart.

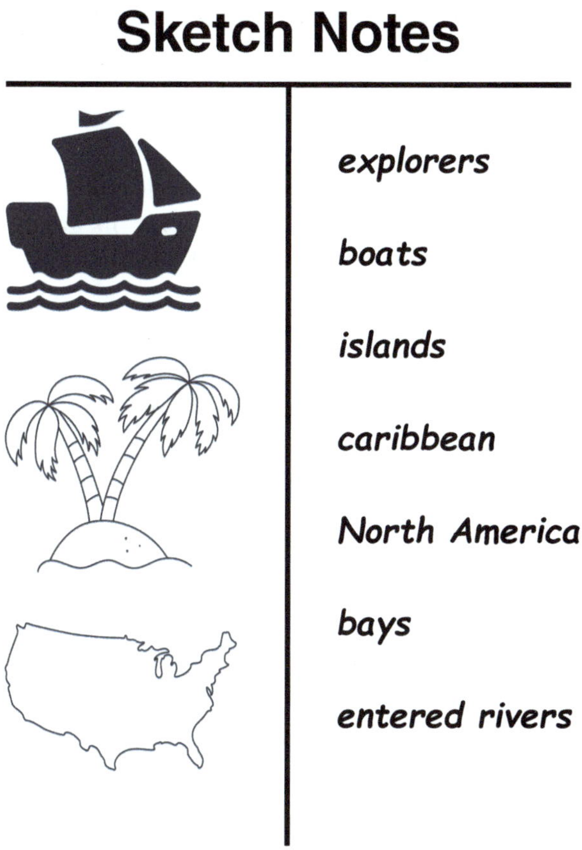

Figure 6.1 An Example of Sketch Notes

At the end of the lecture, the student is given time to write words that describe some of the drawings. These words go on the right. Figure 6.1 is a mock-up of what might be created during a lecture on the Age of Discovery, fifteenth to seventeenth centuries.

It might be helpful to think of classroom adaptations and modifications in terms of Universal Design for Learning (UDL), a teaching approach that seeks to accommodate all students by presenting information in multiple ways, engaging learners in a variety of ways, and providing options for students to demonstrate what they have learned (14).

Am I making things too easy for students when I modify and adapt? Am I somehow inhibiting their ability to accomplish more difficult tasks?

No.

When teachers support students with modifications and accommodations, they are not making the learning "easier" in ways that diminish the growth and potential of students with dyslexia. In fact, they are doing the opposite: through adaptations, teachers give *equitable access* to learning and allow all students to maximize their capabilities. Providing tools like text-to-speech software or audio books or allowing some kids to have more time to read a book or finish a test, gives students with dyslexia (or any reading difficulty) a chance to gain the same content as their peers and demonstrate their understanding in ways that align with their strengths.

When students lack (to greater and lesser extents) certain biological tools to learn reading, teachers provide, especially in the early grades, instruction that builds many of the missing tools. In effect, this is accomplished by "re-wiring" the brain's reading circuit through practices such as repetition, direct and explicit instruction, and systematic and sequential phonics and spelling. Another way to provide missing tools is to give a student an accommodation or modification, thereby enabling them to "work around" their specific deficit. Perhaps an analogy can help us understand the importance of providing these tools.

Picture your educational system as a long sequence of connected rooms. Each room is stuffed with information. Between each room is a door, of a particular color and with a dead bolt lock. To gain access to each room's information, students must pull out their set of colored keys, find the key that matches the door and its lock, and unlock the door for themselves. Once in the room, they can start learning the information from you, their teacher.

Now picture a group of excited students standing outside the very first door. You are standing right there with them, ready to enter the room and teach them the information. Some students are fortunate: they have a key to that door, as well as every upcoming door. But other kids have only some of the keys. Their ability to gain access to the rooms is incomplete. As their teacher, you know this is *not* because they've jumbled or lost their keys. Rather, they never had them in the first place.

You watch as each child steps up, finds the right key, and unlocks the first door. But then a student with no key approaches. What do you do?

You know this student can't easily access the room. What's more, there are other locked doors in their future, doors for which they won't have a key. Your first thought is this: "I should teach them how to break down the door by kicking it. The process will be hard and painful. But if they're successful, they'll gain access and feel empowered because they did it on their own. And maybe they'll be able to kick down all the upcoming doors for which they have no key." You watch as the child painfully kicks at the closed door, over and over again. The door doesn't budge. Then it dawns on you, "Why don't I just *give* them the missing keys?" You do. Then you smile as the student easily unlocks the door, steps into the room, and stands with all the other kids, waiting for you to teach them what they need to know.

In the end, modifications and accommodations are the tools that allow students with dyslexia to get through that locked door of learning. We can let them kick at it for weeks on end with little to no success or simply give them the key they need to get in!

How might I modify my instruction to support students with dyslexia?

Chapter 5 describes teaching techniques that help all students learn, especially those who have dyslexia. The techniques, which include repetition, instant error correction, and direct and explicit instruction, are useful for teaching any content in any grade level. If you haven't historically used these techniques, once you start, you'll have instantly modified your instruction! Here are four more ways to modify your teaching for students who have dyslexia.

Build Peer-Based Supports and Routines

Consider offering support from their class members to all your students. Here are two examples:

- **Reading buddies** involve pairing a student with a lesser reading ability with a student who has greater reading ability. For example, two readers can read the same book together during independent reading time. One key to success is to make sure the discrepancy between the students isn't too large.
- **Peer coaches**, as discussed in J. Samuel's guided Repeated Reading routine. To learn the routine's specific steps and components, revisit Chapter 5 and follow the QR code.

Reduce the Amount of Copying You Ask Students to Do

Instead, provide students with pre-written directions and information. Another way to reduce copying is to teach students to employ a spelling strategy (as described in Chapter 5) other than "visually memorize the correct letter sequence on the board and recreate it on the paper." Options include "think of patterns" and "employ sound–letter associations."

Develop and Maintain Consistent Daily Routines

Routines provide structure and structure is important to all students, especially those who have dyslexia. Daily routines can support areas of study such as phonology, sound–letter learning, spelling-phonics, grammar, shared reading, small group reading, and independent reading and writing.

Incorporate Multi-Modal Activities

Seat work done with paper and pencil is by no means the only game in town. There are plenty of activities that draw on other modalities and that work well with *all* students. Here are two; use your creativity and literacy expertise to come up with others.

Sketch-and-Stretch

To demonstrate comprehension of text in a way other than writing sentences and paragraphs (as in a reading log or journal), students *sketch* their understanding. Sketch-and-Stretch utilizes social learning, movement, and drawn pictures. It also builds background knowledge prior to reading, sets the stage for learning, and works especially well with nonfiction text.

Equipped with a pencil (or pen) and a sketch pad (or clip board with paper), students pair up and stand back-to-back. From the soon-to-be-read classroom text, or from an ancillary text related to the subject matter of the main text, the teacher reads an information rich paragraph to the students. At first, the students simply stand and *listen*. No sketching yet! Then the teacher reads the paragraph again. This time the students sketch pictures that illustrate what they are hearing. When the teacher is done reading and everyone is done sketching, the partners turn to face one another. Student A shows their sketch to Student B and explains it. Student B then shows their sketch to Student A and explains it. If desired, the teacher can repeat the cycle for one more paragraph. Once students know this routine, you'll find that the total time needed for a few paragraphs is less than ten minutes.

Research PowerPoints or iMovies

Written research papers are often assigned in upper elementary and/or middle school grades. To lessen the amount of spelling, writing, and reading inherent in this project, consider allowing students with dyslexia to construct a research PowerPoint, podcast, movie, or even old-school diorama, all of which allow them to demonstrate learning via images, materials, and/or spoken words, rather than written words. Each option can be graded with a rubric. Consider constructing a menu of choices and then offering it to all your students!

Q A Can I modify my instruction by giving students with dyslexia more time?

Absolutely.

Sometimes more time is the only thing that struggling students need. But time is always in short supply in classrooms and there are issues of equity and logistics to consider. Here are a few possibilities for providing extra time to students who need it, especially those who have dyslexia.

- **Provide wait time**. Use wait time in most or all of your lessons. See Chapter 5 for details.
- **Program an extra small group**. If you are skilled at running small groups, consider giving an extra session to those students who need it most. For example, imagine you have created four flexible small groups (A, B, C, D), with the lowest-achieving kids in group A and the highest in group D. Rather than giving each group two twenty-minute sessions per week, give three sessions to the A group and one to the D group. This type of schedule can be run weekly or bi-weekly.
- **Provide intervention time *outside* of general instruction time**. By building dedicated blocks of intervention time into a schedule, schools can ensure students don't miss general education content. For example, a school might build a thirty-minute "Achievement Time" block into the master schedule. All students

do something during this block: some kids go to a reading intervention, some receive a math intervention, and others do extension or enrichment activities.

- **Give more time to complete assignments and tests**. Aside from timed tests that are designed to check the automaticity of a special skill (for example, reading fluency), there is no reason to value speed over fully expressed understanding. Still, providing more time on a test can be tricky to navigate, especially in the upper grades. How and when do you provide time in ways that are equitable? Some teachers offer a chance for *all* students to finish an assessment during study hall, knowing only the students who really need the extra time take it. When extra time for assessments is given to select students, it's typically because they have a 504 plan or IEP that lists this accommodation.

When it comes to giving extra time to take tests, the highly regarded organization Scottish Rite for Children offers a word of caution: "While some students with dyslexia may benefit from additional time, in many cases this does not address the underlying issues that create difficulties for the student. For some students, extra time can cause stress or lead to procrastination" (15).

Regarding tests, what modifications and accommodations can I provide students with dyslexia?

As described earlier, *accommodations* are changes that provide support by changing *how* students access commonly learned information. *Modifications*, meanwhile, are changes to content, assignments, goals, and assessments. Regarding assessments, let's tackle accommodations first.

Remember, with **accommodations**, the only thing changing is how the student demonstrates or reports out on learning. For example:

- Allow a student to move to a study carrel or put on a pair of ear mufflers during test taking.
- Provide a quiet room for taking tests.
- Provide a word bank for typically misspelled words.
- Read test questions aloud to the student.

- Give different ways to respond to test questions, like speaking the answers (and the teacher transcribes them).
- Have students verbalize ideas before writing. This can involve whispering the answer first and then writing it.
- Allow students to speak answers into a speech-to-text application.

Because **modifications** are changes to student goals and expectations, they necessitate changes to assessments. A modified test can look different from other tests, as well as test variations of content.

- Give a multiple-choice format of the test that allows for circling answers rather than filling in blanks with written words.
- Provide sentence starters that show how to begin a written response.
- Give fewer items.
- Grade on what needs to be mastered for that subject. For example, when students write test answers that demonstrate their understanding of text, don't take off points for spelling or grammar errors.

***

In this chapter, we learned that it's important for students (as well as teachers) to understand dyslexia and neurodiversity. When students in a classroom understand neurodiversity, they enter an educated space where they can better support each other. And when people with dyslexia have self-knowledge about their condition, they are in a better position to act, including remembering and fostering their strengths and developing strategies that not only help them learn but also enable them to access support from the adults and systems around them.

Support can take many forms. This chapter focused on teacher-provided accommodations and modifications. Quiet places to read, a shorter spelling list to master, a text-to-speech reader, an opportunity to demonstrate learning in a way other than written words—all are examples of tools that make days in a school classroom less stressful and more equitable. Once teachers know and use these supports, they can also consider them for any student who is experiencing a reading difficulty. As this book has said throughout, we can apply our knowledge of how to help students with dyslexia to the task of helping *all* students learn to read, write, and spell. To greater and lesser extents, what works for a child with dyslexia also works for a child without it!

End of Chapter Resources

1 Faigle, Kevin. 2022. "Neuroscientist's Study Explores How Negative Emotional State Affects Learning." *JAGWire.* Augusta University. https://jagwire.augusta.edu/neurologists-study-explores-how-negative-emotional-state-affects-learning/.

2 Texas State Board of Education. 2024. "The Dyslexia Handbook: Procedures Concerning Dyslexia and Related Disorders." Texas State Board of Education. https://tea.texas.gov/academics/special-student-populations/special-education/texas-dyslexia-handbook.pdf.

3 Scottish Rite for Children. 2023. "Students With Dyslexia Can Benefit From Classroom Accommodations." Scottish Rite for Children. https://scottishriteforchildren.org/students-with-dyslexia-can-benefit-from-classroom-accommodations/.

4 Texas State Board of Education. 2024. "The Dyslexia Handbook: Procedures Concerning Dyslexia and Related Disorders." Texas State Board of Education. https://tea.texas.gov/academics/special-student-populations/special-education/texas-dyslexia-handbook.pdf.

5 Scottish Rite for Children. 2023. "Students With Dyslexia Can Benefit From Classroom Accommodations." Scottish Rite for Children. https://scottishriteforchildren.org/students-with-dyslexia-can-benefit-from-classroom-accommodations/.

6 Pekrun, Reinhard, et al. 2002. "Academic Emotions In Students' Self-Regulated Learning and Achievement: A Program of Qualitative and Quantitative Research." *Educational Psychologist* 37 (2): 91–105.

7 School of College Legal Services of California. 2014. "Term 'Mental Retardation' Changed to 'Intellectual Disability' (K-12)." School of College Legal Services of California. https://sclscal.org/term-mental-retardation-changed-to-intellectual-disability-k-12/#:~:text=On%20October%205%2C%202010%2C%20President,any%20regulation%20that%20used%20the.

8 Reading Rockets. 2024. "Profile: Guinevere Eden." Reading Rockets. www.readingrockets.org/people-and-organizations/guinevere-eden.

9 Reading Rockets. 2024. "Profile: Guinevere Eden." Reading Rockets. www.readingrockets.org/people-and-organizations/guinevere-eden.

10 Loew, Stephen. 2017. "Reading Conditions in Schools: A Review of Fluorescent Lighting, Ultra-White Paper, Unexplained Learning

Difficulties, and Visual Stress in the Classroom." *Journal of Psychology and Education* 12 (2): 85–94. www.rpye.es/pdf/147.pdf.

11 Schiefele, Ulrich, et al. 2016. "Longitudinal Relations Between Reading Motivation and Reading Comprehension in the Early Elementary Grades." *Learning and Individual Differences* 51: 49–58.

12 Guthrie, John, et al. 1990. "Motivational and Cognitive Predictors of Text Comprehension and Reading Amount." *Scientific Studies of Reading* 3 (3): 231–256.

13 McGeown, Sarah, et al. 2015. "The Relationship Between Young Children's Enjoyment of Learning to Read, Reading Attitudes, Confidence and Attainment." *Educational Research* 57 (4): 389–402.

14 Center for Teaching Innovation. 2025. "Universal Design for Learning." Cornell University. https://teaching.cornell.edu/teaching-resources/universal-design-learning.

15 Scottish Rite for Children. 2023. "Students With Dyslexia Can Benefit From Classroom Accommodations." Scottish Rite for Children. https://scottishriteforchildren.org/students-with-dyslexia-can-benefit-from-classroom-accommodations/.

Conclusion

It's a great time to be a reading teacher.

Why? One reason is that reading researchers have clearly identified effective ways to teach students to read, write, and spell. For decades, these hardworking and brilliant thinkers have been deepening our understanding of how our brain's processes give rise to reading, why reading difficulties occur, and what can be done to both prevent and overcome these difficulties. From this knowledge come advances in instructional materials, activities, and teaching techniques. Another reason is this: determined parent groups and advocacy organizations have pushed the field of reading instruction forward, working to make educational and political systems, from schools to states, recognize that dyslexia is a real thing and then create science-based plans to effectively teach students who have it.

Today, in classrooms from Maine to Mississippi, California to Connecticut, dedicated teachers are putting all this hard-won knowledge to use as they teach students to read, write, and spell. Even the students who have the most difficult time mastering foundational literacy skills, such as those with dyslexia, are steadily learning and growing. Evidence-based approaches such as structured literacy are now found in many school districts, transforming the way teachers teach, and powerful classroom tools, such as multi-sensory practices, explicit spelling and phonics instruction, and technology-assisted reading programs, are making teaching more engaging and effective.

This book was crafted to bring some of this knowledge to your attention, collecting in one handy guide information on what dyslexia is, debunking persistent myths that surround the condition, and explaining instructional practices, from phonological and phonics activities to teaching techniques and spelling strategies, that can be brought to bear in daily lessons.

Still, there is always more work to be done, more information to learn, more skills to acquire. Thus, this book is only a beginning, a starting point that recognizes there are plenty of deeper and richer places to go. To that end, I'll conclude with five recommended resources you can dive into. In ways big and small, these resources have been important to me, and I trust that you will find them relevant and enjoyable, too. Some are as current as 2024, while others go way back. Each illuminates how the brain gives rise to reading, why reading difficulties develop, what the complex condition of dyslexia is, and how we can help students learn the reading skills that ultimately help them become happier, more confident people in the world.

Reading research is dynamic, ever deepening, and its connections to classroom practices are constantly unfolding. Meanwhile, teaching is a noble profession, full of dedicated individuals who, melding art, heart, and science, are making the world a better place each and every day. I've always been excited and proud to be a teacher, I hope you are, too, and I wish you the best on your journeys.

ARTICLE

Towards a Dynamic, Comprehensive Conceptualization of Dyslexia

By Maryanne Wolf, Rebecca J. M. Gotlieb, Sohyun An Kim, Veronica Pedroza, Laura V. Rhinehart, Maria Luisa Gorno Tempini, and Sue Sears

Published in the *Annals of Dyslexia* in 2024, this article culminates in a comprehensive, thought-provoking definition of dyslexia. As it winds its way to this definition, it covers a lot of fascinating ground, including a history of dyslexia and an examination of the brain's reading circuit. The article's reference section includes links to a plethora of studies, articles, and books published between 1890 and almost the present day, allowing readers to do a deep dive into whatever area of reading that appeals to them most, from growth mindset and gray matter to developmental dyslexia markers and the poems of Emily Dickinson.

ARTICLE

Ending the Reading Wars: Reading Acquisition from Novice to Expert

By Anne Castles, Kathleen Rastle, and Kate Nation

Originally published in 2018 in *Psychological Science in the Public Interest*, this informative and wide-ranging scholarly article aims to bridge the gap between the states of reading research knowledge and public understanding. Its many components include a comprehensive review of the science of learning to read, an explanation of why phonics instruction is central to learning a writing system (such as English), and an examination of what else children need to be able to do to become expert readers. Especially helpful is a recommended instructional agenda that is balanced, developmentally informed, and based on a deep understanding of how language and writing systems work.

WEBSITE

International Dyslexia Association

With dozens of branches in the United States and Canada, and partner organizations around the world, the more than seventy-year-old International Dyslexia Association (IDA) has a large and long-lasting presence. Its website is a powerful tool, a clearinghouse of resources, reports, trainings, and connections that families, teachers, and researchers can all make use of. The site's "Find Resources" search engine allows users to easily find both general and specific information on a wealth of topics, including structured literacy, science of reading, adult dyslexia, phonemic awareness, classroom accommodations, and policies and legislation that pertain to dyslexia.

BOOK

Proust and the Squid: The Story and Science of the Reading Brain

By Maryanne Wolf (Author)

An oldie but a goodie! Published in 2008 by Penguin, Wolf's book is an informational ode to the human brain, outlining in sometimes great detail how the organ is adaptable, creative, and capable of connecting to other minds through writing and reading. Maryanne Wolf is a polymath in that she's both an excellent writer and a deeply respected and influential reading researcher. She also has a child who has dyslexia and so perhaps sees and understands the condition more intimately than others. For anyone who's a serious reading research nerd, there is plenty of technical talk in this book. Others may choose to skip certain sections and focus on the parts that tell the stories of how written language came to be, how children develop the ability to write and read, and why some have great difficulty mastering skills.

VIDEO

Dyslexia and The Brain

Produced by the nonprofit group, Understood, in conjunction with the Neurodiversity Resource Center, this roughly ten-minute video features dyslexia expert Dr. Guinevere Eden discussing many of the concepts put forth in this book: the parts of the brain used for reading, how the brain integrates these areas so we can read, why people with dyslexia have a difficult time learning to read, and what can be done to help them. Using clear language and simple diagrams, Dr. Eden shows how successful interventions lead to changes in the brain that make reading easier for people with dyslexia. She also highlights what people with dyslexia can sometimes do better than their peers. Once you have viewed the video, you can explore other parts of the Understood website, including the podcasts, web pages, and downloadable PDF fact sheets that have to do with dyslexia.

APPENDIX A

Letter Identification Routine

Lesson Component	*Possible Directions and Language*
Explanation	**Direct and explicit explanation of the objective.** "Today we will learn to name, say the sound, and write the upper and lowercase letter M/m."
Letter Name Identification	**Direct and explicit teaching of the letter and its name.** Point to the uppercase M and say, "This is the uppercase M. Let's name this letter. What letter is this?" Repeat explanation for lowercase. Next, randomly point three times to either of the two letters, asking students to name them.
Letter Sound Identification	**Direct and explicit teaching of the letter and its sound.** Point to the uppercase M and say, "This letter says /m/. Listen, /m/. Say the sound with me." [Students say the sound with the teacher.] Point to the lowercase m and say, "This letter says /m/. Listen, /m/. Say the sound with me." [Students say the sound with the teacher.] Randomly point to one letter or the other, three times in a row, asking children for the sound. "What sound does this letter make?"
Sort the Letters	Show a handful of letters (foam, plastic, or letter tiles) that include three to four uppercase letters (M) and three to four lowercase letters (m). Say, "These are uppercase and lowercase Ms. We will sort them." Place all the letters in the bag. Say, "We will put all the uppercase Ms together and all the lowercase ms together. I will start."

(Continued)

Lesson Component	*Possible Directions and Language*
	Pull out a letter and name it. "This is lowercase m." Pull out an uppercase M and name it. Say, "I will pull more Ms from my bag. If it is an uppercase M, quietly say 'uppercase M.' If it is a lowercase m, quietly say, 'lowercase m'." Pull out letters one at a time. [Students name and teacher sorts into category until all of the letters are done.]
Find the Letters	**Students find the lesson's upper and lowercase letter in text.** This example uses upper and lowercase M/m. The text is a sentence, written on the board or Smartboard or found on the page of a big book, such as "On Monday I saw the moon" or "Are you my mother?" Teacher models the procedure first, scanning through the text, pointing to the target letter, and identifying it. Next, the students scan and identify. When found, letters can be highlighted, circled, underlined, etc. Pacing is brisk.
Write the Letters	The teacher names the lesson's letter (for example, uppercase M), names its component parts (straight lines, angled lines, arcs, etc.), and describes and models how the parts are formed to make the letter. This is followed by student practice using any one or two of a variety of mediums: on paper with a pencil, in the air using sky writing, tracing a sandpaper letter, writing the letter using a dry erase marker and a personal whiteboard. The cycle is repeated for the lowercase version.

APPENDIX B

Word Mapping Template

Word Mapping

Hear It, Say It – say the word. 

Tap It – show each sound of the word.

Spell It – write a letter or letters for each sound.

Read It – slide your finger as you read the word.

Write It – say each letter as you write the word.

APPENDIX C

Sample Lessons for Teaching Foundational Skills

Note: All of the teaching techniques (such as direct and explicit instruction) and some of the activities (such as paintbrush reading and stretching the word) mentioned in the following sample lessons were described in the text of Chapter 5, as well as linked to videos and articles through QR codes. Some activities, such sky writing and palm writing, are demonstrated in videos on my YouTube Channel, Mark Weakland Literacy, and still others are described in Appendix D.

Sample Lesson #1

Objective: Mastering basic sound letter associations (spelling-phonics).
Approximate Time: Thirty minutes

- Warm-up and/or review of previously mastered skills and concepts – five minutes
  - Content examples include phoneme awareness skill such as segmentation, deletion, blending; a specific sound–letter association; the strategy of reading through the entire word.
- Explicit and direct instruction in the new skill—five minutes
  - For example, learning that the/ch/sound is represented by two letters, ch, and that the sound-letters can occur at the beginning of a word or the end of a word.
- Practice in the new skill—ten minutes
  - Practice hearing and reproducing the/ch/sound, forming the digraph ch, spelling the/ch/sound when it occurs at the beginning or end of a one-syllable, closed-syllable word (chin, chop, rich, such, much), reading these words.
  - Multi-sensory instruction, which could include letter tile sorting, tracing with finger over raised or bumpy letters, sky writing or palm writing.

- Connected reading—five minutes
  - Reading and re-reading the ch digraph combination in sentences, such as *Rich hit his chin, How big is an inch, Do not pinch or punch.*
- Cool down—five minutes
  - Orally generating words with the/ch/sound.
  - Orally saying silly sentences that have/ch/words in them. *Chipmunks chew in church.*

Sample Lesson #2

Objective: Mastering more complex spelling-phonic patterns.
Approximate Time: Forty minutes

- Warm-up and/or review of previously mastered skills and concepts—five minutes
  - Content examples include review sound–letter combinations that are "glued together" families (such as *-ung*, *-ink*, *-all*), the strategy of reading through the entire word, the strategy of spelling by analogy, the strategy of "say the word, hum the word" to determine syllables.
- Explicit and direct instruction in the new skill—ten minutes
  - For example, spelling two syllable words using open syllables (*hero*, *baby*, *tofu*) and a combination of open and closed syllables (*robot*, *gumbo*, *relax*).
- Practice in the new skill—ten minutes
  - Practice identifying the syllables in spoken words, spelling segmented syllables and then blending the written syllables into whole words, two-syllable written words between vowel and consonant (*he-ro*) and consonant and consonant (*gum-bo*) to decode them.
  - Multi-sensory instruction might include "stretching" the word by saying it slowly and moving hands, tapping out the syllables of the word, word card sorting, sky writing, or palm writing.
- Reading sentences—ten minutes
  - Reading and re-reading specific words embedded in sentences, such as *Ben does not like gumbo and okra. That baby robot is my hero.*
  - Vocabulary can be built here, with discussion of word meanings (*gumbo*, *okra*), possible pictures that show what the words are, etc.

- Re-reading can be done with formal guided repeated reading procedure, the less formal I Read, We Read, You Read routine, and/or engagement activities like paintbrush reading.
- Cool down—five minutes
  - Writing three words from the lesson, picking out a favorite word, putting the favorite word on a card or sheet, illustrating the word, using it in a sentence.
  - Paintbrush re-reading or flashlight reading.

Sample Lesson #3

Objective: Supporting a student with dyslexia who has strong reading accuracy but needs to build rate/words per minute.
Approximate Time: Fifty minutes

- Warm-up and/or review of previously mastered skills and concepts—ten minutes.
  - Examples of content include sound–letter combinations of "glued together" families (such as *-ung*, *-ink*, *-all*), decoding strategies that address how to break apart words at the syllable level or morphology parts (roots, base words, inflectional endings).
- Practice word spelling and then reading—ten minutes
  - Do a word ladder (to practice patterns, explore word meanings).
  - Next, do a Look, Touch, Say routine. Look for words, look for patterns, and look for meanings. Keep the pace brisk.
  - Finally, read the word list bottom to top and then top to bottom. Keep the pace brisk.
- Read decodable sentences—five minutes
  - Vocabulary can be built here by informally discussing word meanings or showing a picture that illustrates the word.
  - Do a one minute "newscaster" read. Have students reading with confidence, phrasing, and at a rate that is "just right" (not too slow, not too fast).
- Reading from a book—fifteen minutes
  - This book should be of high interest to the student. It does not have to be decodable.
  - Use your teacher sense to determine when to offer instant error correction.
  - Vocabulary can be taught informally.

- Touch on comprehension by occasionally asking and answering questions, predicting, and/or summarizing (among other comprehension skills).

- Guided repeated reading—ten minutes
  - Pick two or three sections of previously read material for re-reading.
  - Re-reading can be done in one or more of the following ways:
    - Formal guided repeated reading procedure.
    - Less formal I Read, We Read, You Read routine.
    - Engaging activities such as paintbrush reading or flashlight reading.

APPENDIX D

Activities for Building Automatic Word Recognition and Fluency

I Read, We Read, You Read (teacher models, choral read, echo read)

Why Do It?

Repeatedly reading the same text builds fluency. Reading fluency is typically associated with comprehension: when fluency goes up, so does comprehension. Reading fluency also allows readers to get through greater amounts of information.

Fluency is a combination of accuracy, rate, and expression. Fluent readers read with a high degree of accuracy, at a good rate of speed (not too fast and not too slow), and with expression and phrasing. Fluent reading sounds like someone talking!

How to Do It!

Say, "We are going to practice this passage a number of times so you can read it fluently. That means you get most if not all of the words right, you read at a steady rate of speed, and you read with expression and phrasing. Your reading should sound like someone talking. I will start by reading and you will follow along as I read."

Identify the sentences, paragraph, or poem that you want the students to read more fluently. As you read the text, have your students follow along, possibly tracking under the words with their finger as you read. Read at a steady rate of speed (not too fast, not too slow) and with expression.

Next, have the students practice the text with you. This is called choral reading. You are reading together! As before, read at a steady rate of speed (not too fast, not too slow) and with expression.

Finally, say, "Now it's your turn to read the sentences. If you need to track with your finger, go ahead. Remember to read like we just did, not too fast and not too slow and with expression."

Paintbrush Reading

Why Do It?

As with I Read, We Read, You Read, paintbrush reading builds automatic word recognition and fluent sentence reading. It's fun, too! As a reminder, fluent readers read with a high degree of accuracy, at a good rate of speed (not too fast and not too slow), and with expression and phrasing.

How to Do It!

Say to your students, "To help you become fluent readers, I'd like you to re-read this passage two more times. If you'd like to use a paintbrush to read, you can. Paintbrush reading helps you read sentences smoothly, in phrases. I will show you how paintbrush reading is done."

Identify the text you want your students to read more fluently. Read the text to them. As you read, pull your paintbrush underneath the words. Read at a steady rate of speed (not too fast, not too slow) and with expression. Show the students how to read in phrases, not word by word.

Say, "Now it's your turn to read the sentences. Remember to read like I just did, not too fast and not too slow and with expression. Use your paintbrush to help you read smoothly, in phrases."

Index

Page numbers in *italics* denote figures.

For Product Safety Concerns and Information,
please contact our EU representative GPSR@taylorandfrancis.com
Taylor & Francis Verlag GmbH, Kaufingerstraße 24,
80331 München, Germany

Printed by Integrated Books International,
United States of America